A Special Gift To You!

From: _____

My Favorite Recipe:

Signed: _____

Date: _____

Seaside
Publishing

P.O. Box 14441
St. Petersburg, FL 33733
Visit our Website at: famousflorida.com
E-mail: sales@famousflorida.com

Manufactured in Canada
ISBN: 0-942084-39-X
Library of Congress Catalog Number: 2001098344
Copyright 2002 by Sandy Freedman

Editorial:
Joyce LaFray

Test Kitchen Director:
Julie Groth

Book Design:
Jennifer Travis

Illustrations:
Kathy Taylor Zimmerman

Cover Photo:
Thomas Bruce Studio

Specialties of the House

Recipes For People On The Go!

by Sandy Freedman

illustrated by Kathy Taylor Zimmerman
book design by Jennifer Travis

Seaside
Publishing

About the Illustrator

Kathy Taylor Zimmerman,
a *St. Petersburg Times* commercial artist for 20 years, is now a noted freelance artist and illustrator.
She has garnered numerous Addy Awards, including an International Bronze 3-D Paper Sculpture
award. Her specialties include whimsical and tropical media with a focus on marine game fish,
especially the elusive snook. She lives in St. Petersburg with her
husband John, daughter Kristi and dachshund, Smedlie.

About the Designer

Jennifer Travis,
has been designing and producing graphic arts for over 20 years. As an employee
of a top-rated Tampa Bay pre-press firm, she has followed the technical art path, from cold
type to high tech publishing. Presently, she resides in St. Petersburg
where she owns and operates her own graphics company.

Dedication

To My Wonderful Family For
Putting Up With Me All These Years!

Table of Contents

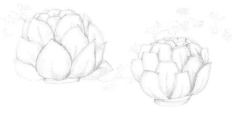

Table of Contents

NOTES FROM THE TEST KITCHEN

Well, what a terrific experience it was preparing these luscious recipes!
I was beginning to get bored with my everyday cooking repertoire when I had the exciting opportunity to test Sandy Freedman's **Specialties of the House**. As soon as I began testing, the process became an adventure. On a daily basis, I was shopping for quality ingredients, testing each unique recipe, and for the best part, I was rewarded with a successful creation every time.

Each and every recipe in this insightful cookbook can be prepared in a myriad of ways. My advice is to be even more creative with these wonderful recipes. If you enjoy more garlic, then add more garlic. If you want to add extra spice, do so. If you prefer to substitute an on-hand ingredient for one that is called for, go right ahead! For sure, these are recipes for people "on the go" like myself, working moms, or dads, single men and women, and busy couples who are looking for simple, easy-to-prepare dishes.

I hope you enjoy the recipes in this cookbook as much as I have testing them.
Here's wishing you a most delicious experience!

Bon Appetit!

Julie Groth

Seaside Test Kitchens

BEGINNINGS

I began this collection of recipes in 1965 when I married my husband Mike. Prior to that time, I rarely cooked. Most of what I made were cookies, omelettes and very basic things, "Cooking 101," if you will. Yet, over the years I discovered that I absolutely **loved** to cook. As I discovered new, exciting recipes, Mike and our growing family became "testers."

Over the years my interest in creating delicious recipes grew. I modified old recipes, experimented with new ideas, and came up with some unique and interesting creations.

A short time after I finished my term as Mayor of Tampa, I had time to cook. It occurred to me that my children — and their children, too — might enjoy preserving these recipes, for future generations of family and friends.

I had difficulty narrowing down the recipes in this cookbook; I have many more, perhaps enough for another book. Incidentally, most of my recipes came from friends, newspapers, magazines, chefs, cooks and many other sources.

Today, I am pleased to share with you my very favorite recipes. It is my wish that my children, their children and others will enjoy this collection for many years to come.

Warmly,

Sandy Freedman

A FEW NOTES FROM SANDY

After almost 35 years of cooking, I would like to share with you a few helpful suggestions which may enhance your culinary adventures.

Fresh herbs are easy to grow and are unique enhancements to any dish. They have the capability to brighten up ordinary foods, and are far more robust than dried herbs. But, if you can't grow your own, or purchase them from your local grocer, do take care to store them correctly. Keep dried herbs away from heat and light; replace them frequently. The flavor of most herbs lasts less than a year. Non-ground spices, such as nutmeg, for instance, can last up to 100 years when kept in their original casings!

As a rule of thumb, use the very best produce, that which is in season. Plan your meals around what's readily available at the market. It will taste better and cost less.

Always have a lemon, or two, on hand. A bowl of lemons on the counter, or table, adds a warm touch to your decor. This age-old fruit lends a fresh taste to many foods. Bottled juice does not compare.

Use the best extra virgin (the first "press") olive oil you can find; it will make a difference in the flavor of your creations. Flavors vary from country to country, and it's fun to try a few from different countries.

Fresh garlic, in my opinion, is the **only** garlic. Once in a while I will use garlic powder, but rarely. Beware of garlic-packed in oil; in most cases it has an odd taste.

In the last few years I've been using kosher salt almost exclusively instead of regular table salt. I keep it in a decorative jar right beside my peppermill, on my counter. And as far as its companion, black pepper, nothing beats freshly-ground. Use a nutmeg or coffee grinder for best results when grinding whole peppercorns.

When a recipe calls for butter, use unsalted; it is better for you, and much more versatile.

In recent years, it's become more important to watch calories and fat. Most times skim, or low-fat milk, reduced-fat sour cream, and low-fat cream cheese and cheeses can be substituted with little difference in taste. "No-fat" products, rarely have a "natural" flavor. Yet, egg substitutes seem to work well in many situations, and are healthier. Occasionally, it works to substitute applesauce for fat when baking.

When in a hurry, frozen pie shells and cake mixes (I love Duncan Hines®) are a real time saver. They can be prepared in a heartbeat, and are delicious. And even better, your guests or family won't have a clue that you "cheated" a little.

Flavored vinegars, such as blueberry or raspberry, or wine, add variety to any salad dressing, and they store well. One of my favorites is sherry wine vinegar. Depending on the style, you're in for a real treat. Don't be afraid to try new vinegars, or make your own.

That wonderful invention called the microwave is good for cooking a number of vegetables, including potatoes. It is excellent for rice dishes such as risotto and for reheating nearly everything. We even use it to soften ice cream. The technology of microwaving has come a long way — why today even browning is possible!

Resealable plastic bags are perfect for marinating a variety of foods. They take up little space in the refrigerator, but be sure to turn them over often so everything inside is marinated well.

Use parchment paper to make baking and roasting much simpler. Purchase the best quality; clean up becomes a breeze!

It may be more costly, but disposable foil pans really are a godsend. Use them for roasting, broiling and even baking. They simplify clean up and can be used for freezing, too. Always keep a supply of sizes on hand.

For entertaining keep track of dinner party menus. Next time you invite someone over you won't have to worry about duplicating a dining experience.

continued

Don't be afraid to experiment using new ingredients — different herbs, some new type of garlic, a drier wine. You may end up bringing that new recipe up a notch. And if there's something in a recipe that you don't like (we don't care for cumin), leave it out, or try a new substitute.

Set an attractive table as often as you can; it makes a somewhat mundane meal taste better. Children probably won't be as likely to wolf down their food, and meals will feel more special.

I wish you the best in your culinary endeavors and hope that these few hints will help to enhance your next dining experience!

Sandy

Appetizers

SAVORY SPINACH BALLS

Here's a make-ahead appetizer that tends to be addictive. These yummy spinach balls can be frozen before baking. Simply place on a cookie sheet and freeze until firm, then remove to a freezer container, or plastic bag. Seal well, store in the freezer for up to one month, then pop in the oven for an instant, delicious appetizer.

1 16-ounce package frozen chopped spinach
2 cups herb stuffing mix
I large onion, finely chopped
4 eggs, well beaten
$^1/_2$ cup Parmesan cheese
$^1/_2$ teaspoon dried thyme
$^1/_2$ teaspoon salt
$^1/_2$ teaspoon freshly ground black pepper
2 garlic cloves, finely minced
$^3/_4$ cup melted unsalted butter

Preheat oven to 350° F. Cook spinach according to package directions; drain spinach very well. Mix all other ingredients together, except the butter. Add butter and mix well. Chill entire mixture until firm enough to form bite-size balls. Roll into small 1" balls and place on greased cookie sheets. Bake for about 20 minutes, or until browned on top. Serve very hot.

Serves: 6 – 8

MOM'S MARINATED SHRIMP

This delicious appetizer, has pleased everyone I make it for. My kids named it after me. If you have leftover shrimp, toss it on the grill for a next-day treat. It always brings raves.

3 - 4 pounds peeled, de-veined and cooked shrimp
2 sliced onions, depending on your taste
1 cup vegetable oil
½ cup fresh lemon juice or white wine vinegar, or a combination of both
¾ cup ketchup
⅓ - ½ cup granulated sugar
3 - 4 cloves garlic, finely minced
½ teaspoon dry mustard
½ teaspoon celery seed
¼ cup minced parsley
Salt and freshly ground pepper to taste
2 thinly sliced lemons or oranges for garnish

Mix all ingredients together in a large non-metallic bowl. Cover and refrigerate, stirring occasionally. This is a wonderful dish as an appetizer, or a main course. It's best after it marinates for a day or so, but be sure to keep refrigerated. Will keep several days.

Serves: 12 – 16 as an appetizer
4 – 6 as a main course

SALMON PÂTÉ

When I prepare this appetizer, I use low-fat cream cheese to save a few calories. But be sure to use a very good brand of canned salmon. Serve with small slices of French bread. It will look very festive served in a hollowed out bread bowl — and it's good for you, too!

2 8-ounce softened blocks of cream cheese (I use low-fat)
1 16-ounce can very good salmon, picked over to eliminate any skin or bones
½ onion, grated
Dash of Worcestershire®
Dash of Tabasco®
Dash of liquid smoke
Salt and pepper to taste

Mix all ingredients well in the containter of a food processor. Adjust seasoning and liquid smoke to your taste. Chill. This will keep a few days if well refrigerated. Great served with French bread. Looks nice in a hollowed out bread bowl, or serve right from a serving bowl.

Serves: 10 – 12

PARMESAN HERB PUFFS

Your guests will think you bought these hors d'oeuvres at the fanciest bakery in town. Every time you serve these luscious puffs, I guarantee you'll get raves. I usually keep a roll on hand in my freezer. Fragrant and savory – they go great with cocktails and melt in your mouth.

**1 17 ¼-ounce package Pepperidge Farm® thawed puff-pastry sheets
(2 pastry sheets),
1 cup fresh grated Parmesan cheese, more if needed
¼ cup fresh chopped herbs: basil, rosemary, and thyme**

On a large work surface or wooden cutting board, sprinkle ¼ cup of the Parmesan cheese together with 1 tablespoon of herbs. Place one sheet of the puff-pastry over the mixture. Sprinkle the top of the pastry sheet evenly with ¼ cup more Parmesan and 1 tablespoon more herbs. Using a rolling pin, roll the pastry sheet into a 12-inch square, making sure Parmesan and herbs are pressed into both sides of the dough.

Roll up one edge to the middle of the pastry sheet. then roll up the parallel edge in the same manner so that they touch in the middle. Press gently to seal together. Wrap them tightly in plastic wrap and chill until firm, about 1 hour. (Can be frozen at this point if wrapped well to use at a later date.) Repeat with remaining pastry sheet, using more Parmesan and herbs if necessary.

Preheat the oven to 400° F. Cover cookie sheet with parchment paper. Cut the chilled, or slightly thawed pastry roll with a sharp knife into ¼ inch thick slices. Place slices 2 inches apart on the sheet. Keep remaining pastry roll chilled until ready for use. Bake in batches in the middle of the oven until tops are golden brown. Gently lift and turn. Bake 8 to 10 minutes more until golden. Cool on rack before serving.
Makes: 3 – 4 dozen

JANE'S HOT ARTICHOKE DIP

I was given this delightful dip recipe while I was attending the University of Miami. It was created by my dear friend Jane Roberts, my surrogate mother. There are dozens of variations of this one, but Jane's basic recipe always seems the best to me.

2 jars of marinated artichoke hearts, rinsed and drained
1 cup freshly grated Parmesan
1 cup mayonnaise
Freshly pressed garlic or garlic salt to taste

Preheat oven to 325° F. Mix artichoke hearts, grated Parmesan, mayonnaise and garlic in the container of a food processor or blender. Pour into a soufflé dish, or small casserole, and bake in preheated oven for about 30 minutes, or till the top begins to brown. Serve hot with cornmeal chips or crackers.

Serves: 4 – 6

AUNT IRIS' SPINACH DIP

Aunt Iris' dip is easy-to-prepare and can be made ahead.
You can also substitute chopped broccoli in place of spinach.

1 10-ounce (1^1/$_2$ cups) package thawed, well-drained chopped spinach
1 3-ounce package dry ranch dressing
1 cup sour cream-regular or low-fat
3 tablespoons mayonnaise
Grated or finely chopped onion to taste

In a medium-size bowl, blend together the spinach, ranch dressing mix, sour cream, mayonnaise and onion. Chill well. Serve in a clear glass serving bowl surrounded with cornmeal chips, crackers, or cut up fresh vegetables. For a unique presentation, serve in a hollowed-out round bread bowl and use the hollowed out bread instead of crackers.

Makes: About 2 cups

MOM'S SPICED PECANS

*These "addictive" pecans work well as a light appetizer, or after dinner
for a special treat. My husband loves an extra dousing of cinnamon.*

1 egg white
1 tablespoon water
1 pound pecan halves
½ cup granulated sugar
1 teaspoon salt
1 - 2 teaspoons cinnamon

Preheat oven to 300° F. In a large mixing bowl, beat egg white and tablespoon of water
until frothy. Add pecan halves and toss well. Set aside.

In small bowl, combine sugar, salt and cinnamon. Add to the pecan mixture and combine
well so that all pecan pieces are coated well. Spread pecans in a single layer on an
ungreased cookie sheet and bake in the oven for about 45 minutes, stirring several
times. Watch carefully so they don't burn. Cool completely and place in
airtight container. These won't keep well in humid weather.

Makes: 4 cups

Salads,
Salad Dressings
& Sauces

APPLE-ARUGULA SALAD

Arugula really gets the taste buds going. It has a peppery flavor that when paired with the sweetness of the apple and the slightly salty Parmesan shavings makes my mouth water. Use a spicy arugula and a good imported Parmesan.

1 bunch of arugula, washed well and stemmed
1 apple, cored, peeled and sliced
$1^1/_3$ tablespoons fresh lemon juice
2 tablespoons extra virgin olive oil
Salt and pepper to taste
Parmesan cheese for garnish
$^1/_2$ cup toasted pecans or walnuts

Dry the arugula well. Arrange arugula and peeled, sliced apples attractively on salad plates. In a small glass bowl combine lemon juice, olive oil and salt and pepper. Drizzle over top with Parmesan shavings and toasted nuts.

Serves: 4

EASY CORN & BEAN SALAD

This salad, great for a crowd, not only tastes good, but is very colorful. The dressing is slightly tangy, but the best part of this recipe is that it is so easy! Add any other veggies that you may desire. Diced zucchini works well.

1 10-ounce can corn, drained
1 10-ounce can kidney beans, rinsed and drained
1 red onion, diced
1 10-ounce can black olive slices, drained
3 large ripe tomatoes, seeded and diced
2 cups Italian dressing
Salt and Pepper to taste

Mix together all ingredients in a large glass salad bowl.
Add in Italian dressing and combine well.

Makes: About 4 cups (1 quart)

SWEET & SOUR CUCUMBERS

I always loved the cool taste of cucumbers, but couldn't eat them until I found the long English, or hot-house varieties which are non-gaseous. Now, they are a staple in my kitchen. The combination of the cider vinegar, sugar and dill flavor creates a salad that goes well with just about any main course.

4 cups cucumber, peeled and thinly sliced
3 tablespoons granulated sugar
$\frac{1}{2}$ teaspoon salt
$\frac{1}{4}$ cup cider vinegar
1 tablespoon chopped fresh dill or 1 tablespoon dried dill
Freshly ground black pepper

Mix the cucumber, sugar and salt together. Stir in the vinegar and dill. Cover and chill at least 2 hours. Add diced tomatoes for a nice variation.

Serves: 6 – 8

OVEN-DRIED TOMATO-MOZZARELLA SALAD

Tomatoes, when oven-dried, become even more delicious. Their intensity of flavor, combined with wonderfully fresh mozzarella, garlic, and pungent basil makes this salad one of my family's all-time favorites. Enjoy as an appetizer, or as a main course. Serve with fresh Tuscan-style bread.

1 pound plum tomatoes, halved
$^3/_4$ cup extra virgin olive oil
2 cloves garlic, minced
1 tablespoon fresh thyme, chopped
1 tablespoon fresh basil, chopped
$^1/_4$ pound fresh mozzarella

Preheat oven to 200° F. Bake the tomato halves, skin-side down on foil, or a parchment-lined baking sheet, for about 2 – 2 ½ hours. Cool, then place tomatoes in a large wide-mouthed jar. Add the olive oil, garlic, thyme and basil and mix carefully. Marinate for 1 hour. To serve, slice mozzarella and place slices in a circle on a large serving plate. Top with the marinated baked tomatoes and drizzle with some of the marinade.

Serves: 4 – 6

GREEK SHRIMP & ORZO SALAD

Oregano makes this dish happen! It's the herb I most associate with Greek specialties. Combined with feta cheese and kalamata olives, it is reminiscent of a meal on a Greek Isle overlooking the beautiful sea. Use Greek oregano if available; we have some of the best in the Greek village of Tarpon Springs here in Florida. This is one of those recipes where you add what you like and eliminate anything you don't.

2 dozen jumbo cooked and peeled shrimp

1/4 cup fresh lemon juice

1/4 cup chopped mint

1 1/2 tablespoons crushed garlic

1 1/2 tablespoons tomato paste

2 tablespoons extra virgin olive oil

1/4 tablespoon each salt and freshly ground black pepper

1 cup cooked orzo

1/2 cup peeled and seeded cucumber

1 tomato, diced

2 green onions, onions (scallions)

1/2 cup pitted and sliced kalamata olives

1/4 cup crumbled reduced fat feta cheese

1 tablespoon chopped fresh oregano

In a large non-metallic bowl, mix together well: lemon juice, mint, garlic, tomato paste, olive oil and salt and pepper to taste. Add the shrimp to another non-metallic bowl and measure in 1/4 cup of the juice mixture. Combine well and allowed shrimp to marinate, refrigerated, for 10-15 minutes. Add to remaining reserved dressing: cooked orzo, cucumber, tomato, green onions and kalamata olives (depending on your taste), feta and oregano. Just before serving, toss vegetable mixture with the marinated shrimp.

Serves: 4

CRUNCHY CHINESE SALAD

I've made a lot of slaw recipes, but I always come back to this one when I want to serve something out of the ordinary. Ramen noodles add a nice crunch to this terrific slaw. The dressing is sweet and tangy.

Salad:
1 head Napa cabbage, chopped
4 green onions (scallions), diced
1/4 cup unsalted butter
2 3-ounce packages ramen noodles
(flavoring packs discarded)
1/2 cup sesame seeds
1/4 cup sliced or slivered almonds

Dressing:
3/4 cup vegetable oil
3 tablespoons low-sodium soy sauce
1/2 cup cider vinegar
3/4 cup granulated sugar

Mix the cabbage and green onions and set aside. Melt the butter in a large heavy saucepan over medium heat. Break ramen noodles into small pieces and brown in the butter for a few minutes. Add in the sesame seeds and almonds and stir to brown. Drain on paper towels and cool.

Mix dressing ingredients together, then microwave for a few minutes to dissolve the sugar. Allow to cool and flavors to meld for about 30 minutes (or make the day before).

Just before serving, gradually add dressing to cabbage and onion mixture until well-coated, but not wet (depends on the size of cabbage).

Serves: 6 – 8

GRILLED CHICKEN & NECTARINE SALAD

The lovely sweetness of nectarines, coupled with the nutty crunch of pine nuts, make this a cut above the ordinary grilled chicken-on-greens. This salad is a perfect warm-weather main course and it's low in calories and fat.

4 skinless boneless chicken breast halves
4 tablespoons fresh lime juice
2 tablespoons fresh chopped thyme or 2 teaspoon dried
1 tablespoon plus 1 tablespoon extra virgin olive oil
1 small clove garlic, minced
5 medium nectarines, thinly sliced (about 2 cup)
6 cups salad greens
1 tablespoon toasted pine nuts
½ cup fresh raspberries

Place chicken is a shallow non-metallic 9" x 9" x 2" glass bowl. Sprinkle with 1 tablespoon lime juice, 1 tablespoon thyme and 1 tablespoon olive oil. Season with salt and pepper. Turn to coat. Cover and refrigerate 1 to 4 hours.

Grill or sauté chicken until golden brown and just cooked through, about 5 minutes per side. Cool. Cut diagonally into slices.

In a medium-size non-metallic bowl, whisk together the lime juice, thyme, olive oil and garlic. Season with salt and pepper. In another bowl, place nectarine slices and add 1 tablespoon of the dressing and toss to coat. Add the salad greens to the large bowl of remaining dressing and toss gently. Divide the greens equally among 4 plates. Add a grilled chicken breast to each dish, then sprinkle with pine nuts and garnish with raspberries.

Serves: 4

NEW POTATO SALAD
WITH
SHAVED PARMESAN

Combine new potatoes with fresh vegetables and there you have it, a delicious salad that will make your guests believe you spent all day in the kitchen. Shaved Parmesan is the crowning touch! If you feel adventurous, use a combination of purple and white potatoes. Yukon gold is also another good substitute. My daughter Lisa loves this salad.

2 pounds small new potatoes, scrubbed
2 pounds trimmed and peeled fresh asparagus
1$1/4$ pounds sugar snap peas
1 bunch chives, cut into 1 inch pieces
$1/4$ cup fresh lemon juice
Salt to taste
$1/2$ tablespoon freshly ground pepper
$1/4$ cup extra virgin olive oil
4 ounces Parmesan cheese, shaved with a vegetable peeler

Simmer potatoes in salted water until tender, about 15-20 minutes. Drain. Blanch asparagus and snap peas, then plunge into ice water to stop their cooking. Drain. Cut asparagus into 1" lengths. Place potatoes, asparagus, peas and chives in a large bowl. Combine gently but well.

In a separate small non-metallic bowl, or salad jar, combine the lemon juice, salt and pepper. Whisk in olive oil, mixing well. Drizzle over the potato mixture and toss gently along with the shaved Parmesan. Serve at room temperature.

Serves: 6 – 8

PURPLE PERUVIAN POTATO, SNAP PEA & MINT SALAD

Crisp, colorful and cool. What more could you ask for? Make sure you use fresh mint — there are many varieties. Purple potatoes are not always easy to find; check out your gourmet grocer. This might be the prettiest potato salad you'll ever make.

1 pound small purple* Peruvian potatoes, or boiling potatoes
1/2 pound sugar snap peas, trimmed
6-8 tablespoons balsamic vinegar
1/4 cup extra virgin olive oil
20 fresh mint leaves, thinly sliced

Cut potatoes into chunks. Cook covered, in a few quarts of cold salted water. Simmer until tender, 15-20 minutes or more. Do not drain the water. Using a slotted spoon transfer potatoes to a colander and cool for 10 minutes. Return the reserved water in the pot to a boil, add the peas and blanch for 1 minute. Drain and refresh under cold water. Pat peas dry with paper towels. Toss peas and potatoes with vinegar, olive oil and fresh mint leaves. Season with salt and pepper to taste.

*Purple potatoes, stain so be careful when you cut them.

Serves: 4

SUMMER COUNTRY SALAD
WITH
FRESH BASIL

Ersatz potato salad with mayo dressing can be very dull. Not so with this inspiring potato salad. The fresh flavor of the basil, coupled with the zesty garlic-like flavor of shallots and a vinegar-based dressing create a light, slightly pungent potato salad. It's good with all kinds of hot and cold meats and poultry. Whenever I make potato salad or coleslaw, I always make enough for a second day, unless I'm making it for a crowd.

2¹/₂ pounds red-skinned new potatoes, quartered
¹/₂ cup Balsamic or red wine vinegar
1 tablespoon Dijon mustard
¹/₄ cup fresh basil, chopped
¹/₄ cup extra virgin olive oil
1 tablespoon shallots, finely chopped
2 tablespoons fresh Italian parsley, chopped
2 tablespoons fresh basil, slivered
Salt and freshly ground pepper to taste

Bring a large pot of water to a boil, then cook potatoes 15-20 minutes, or just until fork tender. Drain and place in a bowl.

Meanwhile, combine vinegar, mustard and basil in the container of a food processor or blender. Process for 15 seconds. With the motor running, slowly add the olive oil through the food tube. Pour mixture over the potatoes. Add salt and pepper and toss well. Fifteen minutes before serving, toss with the shallots, parsley and slivered basil. Serve at room temperature.

Serves: 10 – 12

HONEY-BALSAMIC VINAIGRETTE

This simple, flavorful, vinaigrette is prepared in a snap. Make ahead, but keep refrigerated, then bring to room temperature before serving. Use Florida honey if you have some. Any type of oil may be substituted, but it won't be as delicious.

½ cup balsamic vinegar
½ cup extra virgin olive oil
1 - 2 tablespoons honey
Salt and pepper to taste

Mix all ingredients together well.
For a variation substitute one tablespoon low-sodium soy sauce for the honey.

Makes: 1 cup 1 ounce vinaigrette

SANDY'S RIVER RANCH SLAW
FOR A CROWD

The sweetness of the mandarin oranges and the creaminess of the avocado make this a welcome change from the ordinary slaws we are so used to. If you love ranch dressing, this one's a "keeper." Use dried cherries in place of the oranges, if you wish.

2 10-ounce bags angel hair style slaw
$1/2$ cup sliced green onions (scallions)
$2/3$ cup fat-free ranch dressing
2 4-ounce cans mandarin oranges in light syrup
1 ripe avocado, peeled, pitted and coarsely chopped

Combine slaw and green onion in a very large salad bowl. Add the ranch dressing and toss well. Just before serving, add the remaining ingredients and mix gently. Good for a crowd!

Serves: 12

SALADS, SALAD DRESSINGS & SAUCES

CREAMY ITALIAN DRESSING

This is the perfect all-purpose dressing for various types of salads.
Goes well on greens and potatoes. Try it on coleslaw. It keeps several days in the refrigerator.

$^3/_4$ cup light mayonnaise
$^1/_4$ cup reduced-fat sour cream
2 tablespoons white wine vinegar
1 clove garlic, minced
1 teaspoon fresh chopped basil
1 teaspoon fresh chopped oregano
1 teaspoon Dijon mustard
Pinch of salt
1 tablespoon milk (optional)

In a medium-size bowl combine all ingredients well.
Add 1 tablespoon milk if dressing is too thick for your needs.

Makes: About 1 cup

SWEET POTATOES
WITH
SAGE VINAIGRETTE

Sweet potatoes in a salad will surprise your guests; they will wonder why they weren't so clever. Sage adds a pungent aroma to the other ingredients, while sesame oil lends an Asian touch. This recipe comes from The Inn at Blackberry Farm in Walland, Tennessee, in the foothills of the Smokey Mountains. It's a wonderful place that we've visited several times. Needless to say, it has great food.

8 cups peeled, cubed sweet potatoes (about 4 large potatoes)
2 tablespoons extra virgin olive oil
4 green onions, sliced diagonally (use more if you like)
1 tablespoon sesame seeds, lightly toasted
3 tablespoons champagne vinegar or white wine vinegar
1 tablespoon sugar
2 tablespoons chopped fresh sage
1 tablespoon salt
1/4 tablespoon freshly ground pepper
1/3 cup extra virgin olive oil
2 tablespoons sesame oil
Fresh sage sprigs (optional)

Preheat oven to 450° F. Toss potatoes with the olive oil and place in a foil-lined 15" x 10" x 2" inch pan that has been coated well with cooking spray. Bake for 30-40 minutes, until potatoes are tender.

Transfer potatoes to a large serving bowl and stir in the green onions and sesame seeds. Whisk together the vinegar, sugar, sage, salt and pepper. Gradually whisk in the olive and sesame. Pour over the sweet potato mixture and toss gently. Garnish with fresh sage sprigs, if desired.

Serves: 8

NOTES

Soups

ZUCCHINI & ORZO SOUP

Vegetables and pasta go together as well as any two great foods. You'll love the earthiness of the zucchini with the creaminess of the cooked pasta. A sprinkling of parmesan completes the marriage. This is a wonderful, easy soup. Yellow squash can be substituted for the zucchini, or combined with it.

1 clove garlic, minced
1 onion, chopped fine
2 tablespoon olive oil
1½ cup diced zucchini
2½ cups chicken broth
½ cup orzo pasta
3 tablespoons Parmesan cheese

In a medium-size saucepan, cook garlic and onion in the olive oil until soft; add zucchini and broth. Bring to a boil over high heat. Stir in orzo, boil mixture, stirring occasionally, about 10 minutes. Season with salt and pepper. Ladle into bowls and sprinkle with Parmesan.

Serves: 4

CREAMY WILD RICE SOUP
WITH
SMOKED TURKEY

This velvety soup has the added dimension of earthy wild rice and smoky turkey. Flavors meld perfectly to create a great comfort food. Use fresh turkey for best results.

2 teaspoons unsalted butter
1 cup chopped carrot
1 cup chopped onion
1 cup chopped green onions (scallions)
1 teaspoon chopped fresh or $1/4$ teaspoon dried rosemary
$1/4$ teaspoon fresh ground pepper
3 garlic cloves, minced
2 16-ounce cans fat-free, low sodium chicken broth
$1^1/_2$ cups chopped smoked turkey breast
1 cup uncooked wild rice
$1/3$ cup all-purpose flour
$2^3/_4$ cup low fat milk
2 tablespoons dry sherry
$1/2$ teaspoons salt

Melt the butter in a Dutch oven over medium-high heat. Add carrots, onions, green onions, rosemary, pepper and garlic. Sauté until browned, about 8 minutes. Stir in broth, scraping pan to loosen the browned bits on the bottom. Stir in turkey and rice; bring to a boil. Cover, reduce heat, and simmer 1 hour 15 minutes, or until rice is tender. Lightly spoon flour into a dry measuring cup, leveling with a knife. Make a roux by combining flour and milk in a small bowl, stirring well with a wire whisk. Add to the pan and cook over medium heat until thick, stirring frequently (about 8 minutes). Stir in sherry and salt.

Serves: 6 – 8

PORK & NOODLE SOUP

This soup has a decidedly exotic bent. When you serve it to guests they will experience a taste of Asia. The addition of sherry and soy add richness and a lovely depth of flavor, while cellophane noodles add great texture. In a pinch, you can substitute your favorite pasta, already cooked, in place of the cellophane noodles. For a nice garnish, sprinkle fresh chopped cilantro, or parsley, on top of each bowl of soup.

1 pound lean pork cubes
1 medium carrot, peeled and cut into strip
4 green onions (scallions), cut into ½ inch pieces
2 teaspoons light soy sauce
2 tablespoons dry Spanish sherry
4 cups canned chicken broth, fat-removed
½ teaspoon salt
¼ teaspoon freshly ground pepper
2 ounces cellophane noodles (found in the Asian food section of supermarket)

Combine all of the ingredients, except the cellophane noodles, in a large stockpot and cook over medium heat until the pork and carrots are just tender. About fifteen minutes before serving, place cellophane noodles in a large bowl and cover with boiling water. Let stand for ten minutes. Drain and add to the soup.

Makes: 4 servings

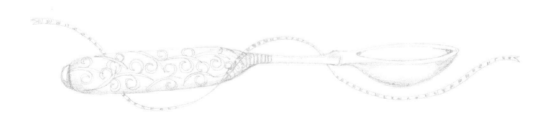

TORTELLINI SOUP

The aroma of fresh basil and savory just-grated Parmesan teases my taste buds for this easy soup. I always purchase the fresh prepared tortellini found in the refrigerated section of the supermarket. They're nearly as good as fresh-from-scratch with little, if any, fuss. Remove the fat by refrigerating the broth for a few hours. Open the can, skim off the fat and you're ready to go.

3 14-ounce cans chicken broth, fat removed
1 9-ounce package refrigerated cheese-filled tortellini
1 $14^1/_2$-ounce can diced tomatoes, undrained
4 green onions (scallions), chopped
2 garlic cloves, minced
2 teaspoons minced fresh basil or 1 teaspoons dried
Parmesan cheese

Bring the chicken broth to a boil in a large saucepan over medium-high heat; add the tortellini, tomatoes, green onions, cloves and basil. Reduce heat and simmer 10 minutes. Ladle into bowls; top with freshly grated Parmesan.

Makes: About 2 quarts

FRESH MUSHROOM SOUP

This is a very basic soup, but a very delicious one!
For variety, add half shitake or oyster mushrooms.

¼ cup chopped onion
2 tablespoons unsalted butter
½ pound diced fresh mushrooms
1 tablespoons all-purpose flour
1 quart chicken stock (may use canned)
1 tablespoon heavy cream
Salt and white pepper to taste
Fresh parsley and chives for garnish

Sauté chopped onion until soft in the butter. Add mushrooms and sauté until slightly brown. Slowly add in the flour. Stir until well combined.
Add chicken stock. Continue simmering until thickened, then add heavy cream, salt and pepper. Ladle into bowls, then top with chopped parsley and chives.

Serves: 4

FRESH MUSHROOM & PASTA SOUP

If you're a mushroom lover too, it's likely you will enjoy experimenting with different varieties. This soup really takes the chill off any cold day. It's hearty, robust and the flavor combination is sure to please. Once you have ladled it into your prettiest soup bowls, try garnishing with a sprinkling of your favorite freshly chopped herbs.

2 tablespoons extra virgin olive oil
1 pound assorted fresh mushrooms, cleaned and sliced
2 10½-ounce cans chicken broth or stock, fat removed
¼ cup small dried pasta, fusilli, works well
Salt and pepper to taste

Heat oil over medium heat in a medium-size saucepan. Sauté mushrooms in the olive oil until soft and slightly browned. Add chicken broth and bring to a boil, then add pasta and continue cooking according to the time on the pasta package. Season with salt and pepper to taste. Serve immediately.

Serves: 4

SKINNY GAZPACHO

This gazpacho is perfect when counting calories. When chilled well, it is my choice for the perfect summer soup. This is a beautiful soup to serve, and so colorful, with the rich redness of vinegrown tomatoes and the green of fresh cucumber. You might try mixing red and yellow tomatoes, making sure they are diced, not mashed together. Serve it in beautiful martini glasses or crystal bowls.

3 very ripe large tomatoes
1 cucumber
1 sweet onion
1 clove garlic
2 cups tomato juice
$\frac{1}{2}$ cup fat-free bottled Italian salad dressing
$\frac{1}{2}$ teaspoons salt
$\frac{1}{4}$ teaspoon fresh ground pepper
Hot sauce to taste
Fresh chopped basil
Fresh cooked whole shrimp for garnish (optional)

Chop all the vegetables and garlic in the container of a food processor or blender until diced, then add in all remaining ingredients except basil and shrimp and blend until a heavy chunked puree. Adjust the seasonings to taste. Pour into nice glass bowls or cups and chill well before serving. Top each serving with chopped fresh chopped basil and a single perfectly cooked shrimp.

Serves: 4 as a first course
2 as a main course

Lunches
& Brunches

DIVINE CHICKEN DIVAN SANDWICHES

This easy-to-prepare sandwich is a take-off on the classic Chicken Divan entrée. It simply melts in your mouth. It makes a perfect light supper with a mesclun of greens served on the side.

4 slices good quality Italian bread
2 tablespoons unsalted butter, softened
$\frac{1}{2}$ pound hot cooked chicken slices
1 10-ounce package frozen chopped broccoli, cooked and drained
1 cup grated Cheddar cheese
Paprika

Preheat oven to 350° F. To make each sandwich, spread each slice of bread with butter and place on a cookie sheet. Bake for about 5 minutes, then top each with slices of chicken, chopped broccoli, Cheddar cheese and a sprinkling of paprika. Return to the oven and bake until the cheese melts and is golden brown.

Serves: 4

GRILLED ONION SANDWICH

An onion lover's delight! Who would ever guess this delicious creation was related to the lily!
Red onions are also excellent in this sandwich and are available year-round.

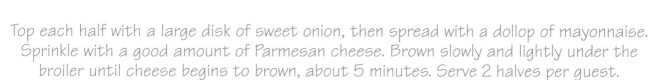

4 English muffins, split and toasted
4 slices sweet onion
$\frac{1}{4}$ cup light or regular mayonnaise
$\frac{1}{4}$ cup Parmesan cheese

Top each half with a large disk of sweet onion, then spread with a dollop of mayonnaise. Sprinkle with a good amount of Parmesan cheese. Brown slowly and lightly under the broiler until cheese begins to brown, about 5 minutes. Serve 2 halves per guest.

Serves: 4

LUNCHES & BRUNCHES

SAUTÉED MUSHROOMS
ON
ENGLISH MUFFINS

Here's an easy, delicious brunch, or dinner dish. Serve with bacon or Canadian bacon, sliced tomatoes and a green vegetable. The Worcestershire adds pizzazz.

4 English muffins, halved and buttered
1 pound cleaned fresh button mushrooms
4 tablespoons butter
$\frac{1}{2}$ teaspoon Worcestershire sauce
Salt and freshly ground pepper to taste
Chopped chives for garnish

Clean and trim a small basket of button mushrooms; slice thinly. In a skillet sauté mushrooms in 4 tablespoons butter, stirring occasionally until they are lightly colored, but still firm. Season with salt, pepper and a dash of Worcestershire sauce. Keep warm while toasting the English muffins. When muffins are browned to your liking, top with the mushrooms. Sprinkle with chopped chives.

Serves: 4

GRILLED PORTOBELLO SANDWICHES

Portobello mushrooms are robust, meaty, and a satisfying substitute for those looking for "burger" substitutes. Use a good aged balsamic and marinate longer for maximum flavor. Paired with focaccia, this recipe makes a delicious, hearty sandwich.

4 Portobello mushrooms, cleaned of stems and black gills
$1/4$ cup balsamic vinegar
$1/4$ cup extra virgin olive oil
1 large garlic clove, minced
$1/4$ cup light or regular mayonnaise
8 3" square focaccia squares

In a medium-size non-metallic bowl, mix together vinegar, olive oil and the minced garlic. Add the Portobello's, toss very gently, then marinate for 30 minutes or longer. Drain off marinade, dry slightly, then grill on outdoor grill, or grill pan until tender. Split the focaccia squares lengthwise and grill the squares until lightly toasted. Spread squares with mayonnaise (you can add herbs to mayo if you desire), top with the Portobello's and add on top-half of focaccia.

Serves: 4

ASPARAGUS, HAM & CHEESE MELTS

The three main ingredients have a natural affinity for each other. Use a fine prosciutto or Virginia ham, fresh baby asparagus and creamy farm-style butter for excellent results.

8 slices thick bakery-style Italian bread
1 cup freshly grated Parmesan
½ cup light or regular mayonnaise
1 pound thin asparagus, blanched
4 tablespoons softened unsalted butter
½ pound medium-sliced premium ham

Preheat broiler. In a medium-size bowl, mix together the grated Parmesan and mayonnaise. Dry blanched asparagus well. Arrange bread slices on cookie sheet and spread a thin layer of butter on each slice. Broil until golden. Turn over each bread slice and top with ham, asparagus and Parmesan mixture to cover the whole top. Broil until golden brown, 1-2 minutes.

Serves: 4

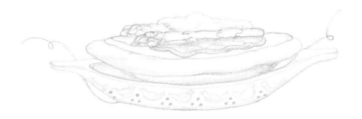

ROASTED TOMATO SANDWICH

Here's an easy way to use my roasted tomatoes in a sandwich (page 112).
When trimmed into small squares they make a great appetizer.

1 loaf Italian bread
4 tablespoons extra virgin olive oil
1 roasted tomato recipe (page 112)
Whole fresh basil leaves
Bunch of arugula
Salt, pepper and Parmesan cheese

Preheat oven to 500° F. Slice bread lengthwise and brush with olive oil. Toast bread until warm, being careful not to burn. Pile on tomato slices, whole basil leaves, arugula, salt and pepper to taste and curls of Parmesan made with a vegetable peeler.
Serve open-faced.

Serves: 4-6

PIZZA CASSEROLE

*If there is one dish that I remember cooking for my children when they young it is this delicious pizza casserole. One bite, and it's like eating pizza — but **we** always thought this was better. Use fresh herbs if you prefer.*

8 ounces sliced pepperoni
1/3 cup melted butter
8 ounces cooked and drained spaghetti
1 cup grated Swiss cheese
1 pound mozzarella, sliced thin
2 8-ounce cans tomato sauce
1 4-ounce can mushroom stems and pieces
1 onion, finely chopped
1 tablespoon dried oregano
1 tablespoon dried basil

Preheat oven to 350° F. Boil pepperoni for 5 minutes in water; drain well. Sauté onion in 1-2 tablespoons butter until golden. Pour remaining butter into a large casserole dish and toss spaghetti in, combine well. Add 1 can of the tomato sauce to the buttered spaghetti, then half of the Swiss cheese, half of the pepperoni, half of the mozzarella and the mushrooms and onions and herbs. Top with the remaining Swiss, pepperoni, tomato sauce and finally the remaining mozzarella. Bake casserole for 20 - 25 minutes, or until bubbly.

Serves: 6

SHIRRED EGGS WITH BACON

Here's an old-style recipe that, once you try, you will keep in your cooking repertoire forever. Great for breakfast, brunch, lunch, or a light supper.

8 slices bacon
Unsalted butter
2 ½ teaspoons bread crumbs
2 tablespoons Parmesan cheese
4 eggs
¼ cup heavy cream
Salt, white pepper and paprika to taste

Preheat the oven to 400° F. Place bacon in a baking pan and cook until well done. Place on paper towels to drain grease. While bacon is cooking, butter an 8" x 8" x 1 ½" square baking dish. Mix bread crumbs and Parmesan together in a medium-size bowl, then press over the bottom and sides of the baking dish. Break eggs 1 at a time into a custard cup, keeping each whole, then carefully pour eggs onto the crumb mixture, placing them evenly over the bottom of the dish. Pour the heavy cream around the egg yolks. Sprinkle all with salt, pepper and paprika to taste. Reduce oven temperature to 350° F. and bake, about 15-20 minutes, or until eggs are just set and bacon is crispy. Serve with steamed vegetables, or a salad of greens.

Serves: 4

BAKED EGGS FORESTIERE

Canadian bacon is so versatile and has such a nice, smoky flavor. Children love to see the cooked eggs placed on top of this luscious casserole. They think they look like bull's-eyes!

4 tablespoons unsalted butter
4 medium slices Canadian bacon, cut into thin strips
$\frac{1}{2}$ cup minced onion
1 pound fresh mushrooms, cleaned and halved
1 tablespoons all-purpose flour
$\frac{1}{2}$ cup chicken broth
$\frac{1}{2}$ cup heavy cream
$\frac{1}{4}$ teaspoon salt
$\frac{1}{4}$ teaspoon freshly ground pepper
6 eggs

Preheat the oven to 375° F. In a medium-size flameproof baking dish, melt the butter over moderate heat. Add the Canadian bacon strips, onion and mushrooms and cook 2 minutes. Sprinkle mixture lightly with flour and cook about 1 minute, until flour is dissolved. Stir in the broth and heavy cream and bring to a boil, then reduce heat to low and simmer 1 minute, stirring often, until mixture becomes thick and smooth and coats the mushrooms. Season with salt and pepper to taste. Crack eggs into the sauce at evenly spaced intervals, then bake for 7-8 minutes in the preheated oven, until eggs are cooked . Sprinkle with fresh parsley. Serve directly from the baking dish.

Serves: 6

BACON & CHEESE PUFF (STRATA)

This is a quiche-like dish affair that always causes a sensation. When puffed up, hot out of the oven with a golden brown top one can simply not resist!

10 - 12 slices bacon
1 - 2 tablespoons unsalted butter
2 onions, chopped
12 slices white bread, each quartered
½ pound Swiss cheese, grated (or a combination of Swiss and Cheddar)
8 eggs
4 cups whole milk
1 teaspoon salt
¼ teaspoon fresh ground pepper

Cook bacon slices until crisp; drain well and crumble. Sauté the onions in a little butter until soft. Arrange half of bread quarters in a single layer in a buttered 11" x 7" x 2" rectangular baking dish. Sprinkle with half the crumbled bacon, half the onions, half the cheese. Repeat, ending with Swiss cheese on the top. Combine the eggs, milk and season with salt and pepper. Mix well and pour over the bacon-onion-cheese combo. Bake in a preheated 375° F. oven until set, puffed, and golden brown (a knife in the center comes out clean), about 50-60 minutes.

Serves: 6 – 8

SUNDAY BRUNCH FRITTATA

The kitchen is filled with lovely aromas on Sunday mornings when this frittata is cooking at our home. It's a visual sensation when it arrives at the table. The Spanish chorizo adds a surprising zing. Grilled, or sliced tomatoes on the side, make a lovely accompaniment.

1 pound assorted mushrooms, cleaned and sliced
1 small Spanish chorizo sausage, diced
8 eggs, beaten (may use egg substitutes)
$1/4$ cup freshly grated Parmesan cheese
$1/8$ teaspoon freshly ground pepper
Olive oil cooking spray

Preheat oven broiler. Heat a large 12" nonstick ovenproof frying pan to medium heat. Spray with cooking spray. When pan becomes hot, add in mushrooms (coat with additional cooking spray if necessary) and cook until soft and lightly browned. Add diced chorizo and cook for 1 minute, then pour in beaten eggs and continue cooking until they are set, pushing back the eggs several times from the sides of the pan with a wooden spoon. When eggs are slightly set, remove from the heat and sprinkle on the Parmesan cheese and ground pepper. Place frying pan under the preheated broiler, about 6 inches from the heat source. Broil until top is lightly brown. Loosen from the pan and turn out onto large round platter. Cut into wedges.

Serves: 4

CHEESY BISCUIT RING

This yummy biscuit dish is loved by kids of all ages. Everybody loves to pull off one of these delicious biscuits from the ring. And it's so easy to make.

2 10-ounce cans of refrigerator biscuits
1 clove crushed garlic
5 teaspoons melted unsalted butter
$^3/_4$ cup freshly grated Parmesan
3 teaspoons chopped parsley, or other herbs

Preheat the oven to 375° F. Grease a bundt pan, or other round cake pan. Separate the biscuits to make a total of 20. Mix the crushed garlic and melted butter and set aside. Mix the Parmesan and parsley and set aside. To assemble, dip biscuits first into butter mixture, then into Parmesan mixture. Place each biscuit around the edge of the pan to make a circle. Bake for 20-25 minutes, or until brown.

Serves: 4 – 8

LUNCHES & BRUNCHES

HERBED BISCUIT RING

A mixture of aromatic herbs instills a savory taste in these ready-made biscuits. And it works well for any occasion. Place the ring on a tray with sprigs of the herbs for a pleasant presentation. If you prefer, use your favorite herbs instead of sage.

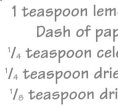

1 10-ounce can of refrigerator biscuits
3 teaspoons unsalted butter, softened
1 teaspoon lemon juice
Dash of paprika
$\frac{1}{4}$ teaspoon celery seed
$\frac{1}{4}$ teaspoon dried thyme
$\frac{1}{8}$ teaspoon dried sage

Preheat oven to 400° F. In a small non-metallic bowl, blend together butter, lemon juice, paprika, celery seed, thyme and dried sage to make an herb butter. Separate the biscuits and spread the top of each biscuit with the herb butter. Arrange them in a round pie pan or other round pan, buttered side up, in a slightly overlapping ring. Bake for 15-18 minutes until golden.

Serves: 4 – 6

Poultry

QUICK GARLICKY CHICKEN

My family loves garlic and lots of it; the amount you use should fit your personal taste buds. This "quicky" is simply scrumptious. Add more garlic if you dare!

4 6-ounce skinless, boneless chicken breasts
5 tablespoons extra virgin olive oil
Salt and pepper to taste
10 peeled cloves of garlic

Preheat oven to 425° F. Arrange the chicken breasts in a baking dish and drizzle with olive oil. Turn to coat. Season with salt and pepper. Scatter garlic cloves over the chicken. Cover and bake for 20 minutes. Uncover and bake 10 minutes more at an increased
temperature of 450° F.

Serves: 4

GARLIC OVEN-FRIED CHICKEN BREASTS

Everyone loves fried chicken. By being baked this version cuts calories and fat. Surprisingly, the flavor doesn't suffer one bit. The creamy roasted garlic and herbs make it very special indeed!

1 whole head of garlic
Cooking spray
1½ cup dried bread crumbs
3 tablespoons chopped fresh thyme
2 tablespoons chopped fresh sage
2 tablespoons chopped fresh rosemary
1 tablespoon dry mustard, such as Coleman's®

Pinch cayenne pepper
1 teaspoon salt
¼ teaspoon fresh ground pepper
1½ teaspoons extra virgin olive oil
6 skinless chicken breast halves, bone in
5 large egg whites

Preheat the oven to 425° F. Spray the garlic head with the cooking spray; place in a small ceramic or clay baking dish and cover with foil. Bake until very soft, about 50-60 minutes. Remove from the oven and allow to cool, then cut top of the garlic head off and squeeze roasted garlic into a small dish. Set aside.

Increase the oven temperature to 500° F. Mix the bread crumbs, herbs, spices, salt and pepper in a medium-size bowl. Using your (clean) fingers, mix in the olive oil and blend well.

Spread a thin even layer of the garlic over each chicken breast. In a separate medium-size bowl, whisk the egg whites until foamy, then dip the chicken breasts into the whites coating evenly, then coat with the prepared crumb mixture. Place on a rack in a roasting pan and bake in pre-heated oven for about 15 minutes. Remove from the oven and spray with water, using a spray bottle, to slightly moisten. (This is necessary to make a crispy crust.) Return chicken to oven and bake until golden and crisp, about 15-20 minutes more. Allow chicken to cool. You can cut each piece in half, if desired. Chill until ready to serve.

Serves: 6

BLASTED CHICKEN

This dish will blast your guests into pure delight. Amazingly easy and delicious. It comes out juicy and just right every time.

1 3¹/₂ pound rinsed and dried chicken
Salt and pepper
Herbs of choice (rosemary, garlic, oregano, etc.)

Preheat the oven to 450° F. Season the rinsed and dried chicken well all over, including the cavity with salt and pepper (add herbs if you like). Place in a heavy roasting pan.

Roast for about 45 minutes, or until the juices run clear when the thigh is pricked with the tines of a fork. Transfer to a plate and let rest 15 minutes before slicing.

Serves: 4

HERB-CRUSTED CHICKEN

Here's another easy-to-prepare oven-fried chicken dish. Add fresh garlic to the olive oil if you want even more flavor. It can be prepared with your favorite chicken parts and if you prefer, served atop a mesclun of greens. Close your eyes now, taste those great herbs and spices!

4 6-ounce boneless, skinless chicken breasts
³/₄ cup fresh breadcrumbs
1 teaspoon fresh thyme, chopped
1 teaspoon fresh basil, chopped
1 teaspoon fresh marjoram, chopped
1 pinch of cayenne pepper
1 egg white, lightly beaten
1 teaspoon extra virgin olive oil
Salt and pepper to taste

Preheat oven to 400° F. In a large bowl, mix together bread crumbs, thyme, basil, marjoram, cayenne pepper and salt and pepper. Using a pastry brush, brush the top of each chicken breast with the beaten egg white, then press top side of each piece into the crumb mixture.

Heat olive oil in a medium-size sauté pan, then, when oil is hot, carefully add chicken breasts with breaded side down. Sauté over moderately high heat until brown, about 1 minute. DO NOT TURN. Remove from the heat and place chicken breasts, breaded sides up, on greased 9" x 9" x 2" baking pan. Bake for about 15-20 minutes, or until done, when juices run clear when pricked with the tines of a fork.

Serves: 4

"OUT OF THIS WORLD" WINGS

When asked my opinion, I would have to tell you that chicken wings (done right) are downright nearly decadent. They are so juicy and gooey. Of course they have a little more fat, but (once in a while) they are well worth the splurge. They just melt in your mouth.
A superb hors d'oeuvre, or main course.

24 chicken drumettes
1 cup low-sodium soy sauce
1/2 cup dry red wine
1/2 cup plus 1 tablespoon honey
1/4 teaspoon fresh grated gingerroot

Preheat the oven to 400° F. Arrange wings skin side down in a roasting pan, in one layer. In a medium-size saucepan, heat the remaining ingredients over moderately low heat, stirring slowly until the sugar is dissolved. Pour over the wings.

Place in the middle of the oven and bake for about 45 minutes. Turn the wings over and bake until liquid is thick and sticky, 45-60 minutes more. Wings should be very brown, but not burned.

Serves: 4 (6 wings each)

LIME, APRICOT & SOY SAUCE CHICKEN WINGS

Three main ingredients each add a unique flavor to the wings: citrus, sweet and tangy. All wrapped up in yummy wings. Easy, and very "Florida" with the tropical lime taste.

5 pounds chicken wings
$\frac{1}{2}$ cup fresh lime juice
$\frac{1}{2}$ cup apricot preserves
$\frac{1}{2}$ cup low-sodium soy sauce
$\frac{1}{3}$ cup granulated sugar
2 large garlic cloves

Preheat the oven to 425° F. Halve the wings, cut off the little tips and discard. Divide into single layers between 2 9" x 9" x 2" baking pans. Combine lime juice, preserves, soy sauce, sugar and garlic cloves in container of a food processor or blender and pour over the wings to cover all parts. Bake about 45 minutes, then turn wings and bake another 45 minutes, or until the liquid is thick and syrupy.

Serves: 4 – 6

PICNIC LEMON & BASIL CHICKEN

This chicken is so flavorful with the lemon and basil leaves under the skin. Mmmm good!!. It is lovely served cold, or at room temperature. I always make a double batch to have some the next day. Great for a picnic!

4 chicken breast halves, fat trimmed
Salt and pepper to taste
4 large basil leaves
4 garlic cloves, bruised with the back of a knife
8 thin lemon slices
1 tablespoon extra virgin olive oil

Preheat the oven to 400° F. Place the chicken pieces in a baking dish and sprinkle well, top and bottom, with salt and pepper. Arrange in a 9" x 9" x 2" baking dish, skin side up. Loosen the skin from each chicken piece, slipping a basil leaf between the skin and the meat. Then add the garlic cloves to the baking dish and place a slice of lemon on top of each piece. Drizzle chicken with olive oil. Bake, basting occasionally and turning the chicken and the dish occasionally, 35-45 minutes until browned. Garnish each with the remaining lemon slices and clove of fresh roasted garlic.

Serves: 4

LEMON CHICKEN LEGS
WITH
GARLIC AND ROSEMARY

Chicken legs are comfort food, yet they take on a special appeal with the lemon, garlic and rosemary. Not "your mother's" chicken legs, to be sure.

4 whole chicken legs (thigh and drumstick)
2 lemons, halved
2 tablespoons minced fresh rosemary
2 tablespoons extra virgin olive oil
2 garlic cloves, minced
6 tablespoons water

Pat chicken dry and rub all over with 2 of the lemon halves. Season with salt and pepper and half of the rosemary.

In a heavy skillet, heat the oil over moderately high heat and sauté chicken, skin side down, 7 minutes until golden brown. Turn and squeeze juice from the remaining 2 lemon halves over the chicken. Cook, covered, over moderately low heat 30 minutes more, or until cooked through.

Transfer the chicken to two plates and cover with foil to keep warm. Add garlic and remaining rosemary to the pan. Sauté until garlic is just golden. Add water, scraping to loosen brown bits on the bottom of the pan; simmer 1 minute. Drizzle sauce over the chicken.

Serves: 4

AUNT BINNIE'S CHICKEN

Sweet apricot preserves and teriyaki sauce combine to form a sweet, yet tangy marinade.
Sesame seeds add a lovely crunchy crispy taste to the chicken. My tester, Julie,
loved the pungent taste; so did her year-old daughter Alex.

1 3-4 pound large chicken, cut up, cleaned and well dried
1 10-ounce jar of apricot or peach preserves
2 tablespoons teriyaki sauce
2 tablespoons red wine vinegar
$\frac{1}{2}$ cup sesame seeds

Blend apricot preserves, teriyaki sauce and red wine vinegar in a small bowl. Place chicken parts in a plastic resealable bag, pour in the prepared sauce, shake and mix well then marinate about 8 hours, or overnight. You may also do this in a large glass bowl. Mix several times during the marinating process.

When ready to cook, preheat oven to 400° F. Remove chicken from the marinade, reserving the marinade; then place chicken parts in one or more large baking dishes in a single layer. Pour reserved marinade over all. Bake for about 45-50 minutes, being careful chicken doesn't get too brown. Cover with foil if chicken begins to brown.

Remove chicken from oven, then sprinkle sesame seeds over all. Return to the oven and bake, uncovered, 15 minutes more, or until sesame seeds and chicken are brown.

Serves: 4 – 6

SAUTÉED BREASTS OF CHICKEN

There is a refined sophistication to this entree which will make your guests think you slaved all afternoon. This recipe seems like a big production, but really isn't!

4 skinless, boneless chicken breast halves
Salt and Pepper
All-purpose flour
5 tablespoons butter
4 cups chopped onions
6 laurel (bay) leaves
1 large fresh thyme sprig or $\frac{1}{4}$ tablespoon dried
1 $14\frac{1}{2}$ -ounces can low-sodium chicken broth
$\frac{3}{4}$ cup dry white wine
4 large garlic cloves, minced

Sprinkle the chicken with salt and pepper to taste. Coat it generously with flour; shake off excess. Melt 2 tablespoon butter in a large skillet over medium-high heat. Add the chicken and sauté until golden brown, but not cooked through, about 2 minutes per side. Transfer chicken breasts to a plate.

In the same skillet, over medium heat, melt 1 tablespoon butter. Add in the chopped onions, bay leaves and fresh thyme, then sauté until onions are tender, about 10 minutes. Increase the heat to "high," add the broth, wine and garlic. Bring to a boil and cook until liquid is reduced by half, about 6 minutes.

Add chicken to the pan; turn to coat in the wine mixture. Reduce heat to low; cover and simmer until chicken is cooked through, about 5 minutes. Remove chicken from pan onto a platter; cover with foil to keep warm. Strain the sauce and reserve half of the onions. Return sauce to the pan with the reserved onions and bring to a simmer. Add the remaining 2 tablespoon butter and whisk until just melted. Season with salt and pepper; spoon sauce over the chicken.

Serves: 4

CRISPY APRICOT DUCKLING

We love duckling and prefer the apricot flavoring to the traditional black cherry or orange versions. Don't be afraid to try this easy dish.

1 Long Island duckling,* defrosted
2 teaspoons salt
1/2 teaspoon fresh ground pepper
1/4 cup apricot liqueur or brandy
1/4 cup apricot preserves

Preheat oven to 450° F. Clean duckling well, according to directions, being sure to remove giblets from the cavity. Rinse well. Pat dry with paper towels. Season all over (and in the cavity) with salt and pepper.

Place duck on rack in a heavy roasting pan and bake for about 20 minutes. During that time, prick the duck all over with a fork several times to drain off the fat. Remove from the oven and pour the apricot liqueur, or brandy, over the duck. Lower the temperature of the oven to 350° F. and roast the duckling for 1 1/2 hours more, being sure to prick the skin all over several times during this period. Remove duckling from the oven and coat with the apricot preserves; return to the oven for about 15 minutes more. If duck begins to get too brown during roasting time cover loosely with foil, being sure it is uncovered for the last 15 minutes. Cut into 2 or 4 pieces, depending upon your appetite.

* You may substitute any other quality duckling.

Serves: 2 – 4

GRILLING SAUCE

This sauce is great for any kind of poultry, or meat. It wakes up my taste buds, but doesn't overwhelm them. There's a bit of sweet, citrus and spice, but no fat. It's certainly easy and versatile.

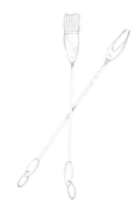

$1/4$ cup packed brown sugar
$1/4$ cup teriyaki sauce
$1/4$ cup orange juice
$1/4$ cup ketchup

Combine all ingredients. Brush on before grilling.

Makes: 1 cup

PEACH & GINGER SALSA

Peach and ginger are the perfect combination to produce this lively sauce.
It is very good with chicken, fish, or toasted tortilla chips.

1 cup peeled and cubed peaches (about 2 peaches)
1 cup cubed seeded tomato, about 3 tomatoes
$1/4$ cup sliced green onions (scallions)
$1^1/_2$ tablespoons granulated sugar
2 tablespoons cider vinegar
1 tablespoon minced peeled fresh ginger
1 teaspoon salt
Freshly ground pepper to taste

Combine all ingredients and stir very well. Let rest at least one hour
for flavors to marry.

Makes: About 2$^1/_2$ cups

Seafood & Shellfish

ROASTED FISH FILLETS
WITH
FRESH DILL

In addition to being low in fat and high in flavor, this dish is very versatile. It is a lovely presentation: golden fish, bright green spinach, yellow lemon wedges and bright red yellow bells.

non-stick vegetable oil spray

4 6-ounce fish fillets of snapper, flounder, catfish or other firm white fish

1 tablespoon fresh squeezed lemon juice

4 teaspoons Dijon mustard

1/2 cup finely chopped fresh dill

1 pound cooked fresh spinach

1 tablespoon minced fresh garlic

Lemon wedges

Cherry tomatoes

Preheat oven to 450° F. Spray large ovenproof baking dish with the non-stick vegetable oil spray. Arrange fish fillets in the dish; sprinkle with the lemon juice and spread 1 teaspoon Dijon mustard on each filet. Sprinkle with the chopped dill. Bake until fish is cooked through, about 10 minutes. Arrange each fillet atop a bed of lightly sautéed fresh spinach that has been cooked with a little minced garlic. Add lemon wedges and cherry tomatoes alongside.

Serves: 4

HEAVENLY BROILED GROUPER

A quality mayonnaise, green onions, and fresh Parmesan combine to make these fillets a cut above the ordinary. You can use any firm white fish; grouper just happens to be one of my favorites.

6 6-ounce fresh Grouper fillets
2 tablespoons fresh lemon juice
$1/2$ cup fresh grated Parmesan cheese
$1/4$ cup softened unsalted butter
3 tablespoons mayonnaise (can use reduced-fat style)
3 tablespoons chopped green onions (scallions)
$1/4$ tablespoon salt
Dash of Tabasco sauce

Preheat oven broiler. Place fish fillets in a single layer in a well-greased baking pan, or Pyrex dish. Brush generously with lemon juice and allow to stand for about 10 minutes.
In a small glass bowl, combine the remaining ingredients and set aside.
Broil the filets about four inches from broiler flame, for 6 - 8 minutes. Remove from oven. Spread with the prepared cheese-mayonnaise mixture. Broil 2-3 minutes more, or until lightly browned.

Serves: 6 6–ounce fish fillets

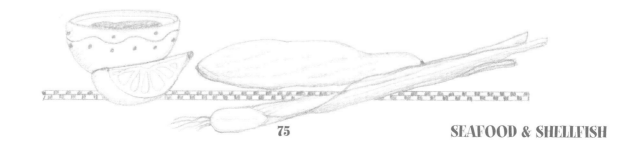

SEAFOOD & SHELLFISH

SNAPPER PROVENÇALE

In Provence, the magnificent area in southern France, many local dishes frequently use the ingredients in this recipe. Ripe tomatoes and fragrant onions enhance the flavors of the snapper. Add some garlic to zip things up. If you're fish lovers, this dish will become a family favorite.

4 6-ounce red snapper fillets, skinned
2 tablespoons extra virgin olive oil
$\frac{1}{2}$ teaspoon sea salt or kosher salt
$\frac{1}{4}$ teaspoon freshly ground pepper
$14\frac{1}{2}$-ounce can sliced tomatoes, drained
1 onion, sliced
1 lemon cut into 4 wedges
Freshly chopped parsley

Preheat broiler. Sprinkle salt and pepper on both sides of the snapper filets. Place on greased broiler pan and drizzle with 1 tablespoon olive oil. Broil 4 minutes. Remove from the oven, turn the fillets and top with tomato and onion slices. Drizzle with remaining 1 tablespoon olive oil. Broil 4-5 minutes more, or until fish just begins to flake when touched with a fork. Garnish with lemon wedges and chopped parsley. Serve with fluffy rice and a green salad or vegetable

Serves: 4 6–ounce servings

GLAZED ASIAN-STYLE SALMON

Salmon is one of the most versatile fish; it is also one of the best values. This recipe combines the best in Asian flavor with the lovely, subtle flavor of brown sugar. It's good over rice, or atop a salad.

6   4-6 ounce salmon fillets, skinned
¼ cup low-sodium soy sauce
3 garlic cloves, chopped
3 tablespoons light brown sugar
2 tablespoons honey
1 tablespoon water
1 tablespoon extra virgin olive oil
1 tablespoon fresh basil or parsley

Preheat oven to 400° F. Spray a heavy baking pan evenly with cooking spray. Trim salmon to desired shape.

Combine all of the other ingredients in a medium-size bowl and mix until well blended. Place the salmon fillets in the prepared baking pan. Brush each fillet well with the marinade. Bake, basting with marinade at least twice until salmon begins to flake when gently pressed.

Serves: 6

SEAFOOD & SHELLFISH

BAKED SALMON
WITH
MUSTARD-DILL SAUCE

*Dill is a natural partner for salmon. It makes a slightly piquant
sauce when paired with sour cream and Dijon mustard.*

1¹/₂ pounds center cut salmon fillet, skin on
1 cup sour cream, regular or low-fat
¹/₄ cup fresh chopped dill
3 tablespoons finely chopped onion
2 tablespoons Dijon mustard
Salt and pepper to taste
2 tablespoons minced garlic

Preheat oven to 400° F. Lightly oil, or spray a baking sheet with oil.
In a small bowl whisk together the sour cream, dill, onions, Dijon mustard and salt and
pepper to taste. Allow to stand a few moments so flavors meld. Place the salmon filet
skin side down on the baking sheet. Sprinkle with 2 tablespoons minced garlic, salt and
pepper, then spread with one-third cup of the sour cream mixture. Bake for about 20
minutes, or until salmon flakes. Serve with the remaining sauce.

Serves: 4 – 6

SALMON
WITH
FRESH CITRUS VINAIGRETTE

The crisp, clean flavor of citrus combined with garlic and fresh herbs makes this dish a mouth-watering delight. Extra virgin olive oil adds flavor, but regular olive oil will do just fine.

1½ pounds fresh salmon fillets, skinned
1 clove garlic, crushed
¼ cup fresh Florida orange juice
2 tablespoons fresh parsley, chopped
2 tablespoons fresh basil, chopped
2 tablespoons fresh mint, chopped
2 tablespoons balsamic vinegar
1 tablespoon Dijon mustard
1 tablespoon extra virgin olive oil
1 tablespoon minced shallots
Salt and pepper to taste

Preheat oven to 450° F. Trim salmon into six 4-ounce servings. To make a vinaigrette, blend all remaining ingredients in a medium-size non-metallic bowl. Allow flavors to meld for a few minutes.

Place the salmon fillets in a foil-lined baking pan and spoon a little of the vinaigrette over the each fillet. Bake just until salmon begins to flake when touched. Spoon the remaining sauce over each serving of fish.

Makes: 6 4-ounce servings

SEAFOOD & SHELLFISH

SANDY'S CATFISH FILLETS
WITH
TROPICAL SALSA

Catfish is a lovely white fish that is very sweet and somewhat delicate tasting. Even kids like this mild fish! I especially like to serve catfish with my tropical salsa which adds color and sweetness to the dish. Add more jalapeno to turn up the heat.

Catfish:
4 6-8 ounce farm-raised catfish fillets
Butter-flavored cooking spray
Paul Prudhomme's Blackened Redfish Magic®
Seasoning Blend

Salsa:
1 ripe mango, peeled and chopped
1 ripe avocado, peeled and chopped
1 cup pineapple, peeled and chopped
1 ripe tomato, seeded and chopped
1 fresh jalapeno pepper, seeded and finely minced
2 green onions (scallions), finely sliced
Juice of $\frac{1}{2}$ lemon
$\frac{1}{4}$ cup extra virgin olive oil
Small amount of sugar to taste

Heat a non-stick pan over medium-high heat. Rinse each fillet and pat dry. Spray each side with the cooking spray and season with the Paul Prudhomme Redfish Magic (this is spicy so use according to your taste.) Place each fillet in the heated pan and sauté until brown. Turn each fillet and continue cooking till fish just begins to flake when touched with a fork. Serve with lemon wedges.

To prepare the salsa, combine mango, avocado, pineapple, tomato, jalapeno and green onion. Add the lemon juice, olive oil and sugar to taste. Mix well.
Taste and adjust seasonings. Chill.

Makes: 3 cups

BASIL SHRIMP

No herb has quite the fragrance and flavor of fresh-picked basil. It lifts the flavor of the shrimp while the fresh garlic add a nice little zing. Use a good French vermouth.

1 pound large (21-30) shrimp, shelled, deveined and butterflied, tails on
½ cup extra-virgin olive oil
2 large cloves of garlic, minced
¾ cup fresh basil, finely chopped
3 tablespoons white dry vermouth
4 tablespoons lemon juice
Salt and pepper to taste
1 cup cherry tomatoes
6 lemon slices
1 bunch whole basil leaves

Heat olive oil in a medium-large sauté pan over medium heat. Add garlic, chopped basil, vermouth and lemon juice. Add the shrimp to the pan and sauté, stirring constantly, for about two to four minutes, or until pink. Add salt and pepper to taste.

Transfer to a glass mixing bowl and chill for one to two hours. Serve at room temperature by skewering the shrimp alternating with cherry tomatoes. Garnish with lemon slices and whole basil leaves.

Serves: 4

SEAFOOD & SHELLFISH

SAUTÉED SCALLOPS
WITH
ROSEMARY AND FRESH LEMON

There is nothing quite like the flavor of fresh lemon to bring out the innate sweetness of the scallops. Rosemary adds an unexpected plus.

1 pound small scallops, rinsed and dried
¼ cup extra virgin olive oil
2 medium-size garlic cloves, thinly sliced
1½ tablespoons whole fresh rosemary
Salt and pepper to taste
1½ tablespoons fresh lemon
Rosemary sprigs for garnish

Heat the extra virgin olive oil and garlic together in a medium-size skillet over moderate heat. Stir occasionally until the garlic is pale golden; be careful not to burn. Turn up the flame and stir in the rosemary. Add the scallops in a single layer, then season with salt and pepper and cook until opaque, about two to three minutes. Using a slotted spoon, transfer scallops to a small bowl.

Add the lemon juice to the skillet drippings and simmer until the liquid is reduced to a syrupy glaze. Return the reserved scallops and any accumulated juices to the pan; toss to coat with the glaze. Heat through and serve. Garnish with rosemary.

Serves: 4

SOUR CREAM DIJON MUSTARD SAUCE

This lovely sauce is a cinch to make. It goes well with grilled salmon or other fish.
Use lime juice for a change of pace.

1 cup sour cream
$\frac{1}{2}$ cup Dijon mustard
$\frac{1}{2}$ cup fresh lemon juice
4 cloves minced garlic
2 tablespoons dried dill

In a non-metallic bowl, combine all ingredients well. Refrigerate until chilled.
When ready to serve, bring almost to room temperature.

Makes: 2 cups

NOTES

Meats & Main Dishes

SOUTHWESTERN BRISKET

Many people have never eaten brisket of beef. One taste and they become brisket lovers. It cooks up very tender, but is better the next day after the meat absorbs the lovely flavors of the onions, chili sauce and brown sugar. This is one of those dishes that can be made the day before and reheated. Kids love it in sandwiches.

3 - 4 pounds beef brisket
5 onions, thinly sliced
$\frac{1}{2}$ cup cold water
$\frac{1}{2}$ cup chili sauce
2 tablespoons light brown sugar
1$\frac{1}{2}$ tablespoons vinegar
Dash of Worcestershire sauce

Preheat the oven to 325° F. In a large, heavy sauté pan, sear the beef brisket, browning well on both sides. Place in a large roasting pan and smother with the onions. Mix all remaining ingredients together and pour over the beef with onions. Cover and bake for about 2$\frac{1}{2}$ hours, or until the meat is easily pierced with a fork. Cool and slice against the grain. Serve the sauce as gravy in an attractive gravy boat.

Serves: 6 – 8 or more

GRILLED FLANK STEAK
WITH
ROSEMARY

Lots of garlic and rosemary make the flank steak taste great. I love it sliced thin, piled onto good bread with a slathering of mayonnaise. Flank steak is a wonderful cut because it cooks quickly and marinating makes it more tender and flavorful. Always great the next day for sandwiches, in a pasta salad, or atop a bed of greens.

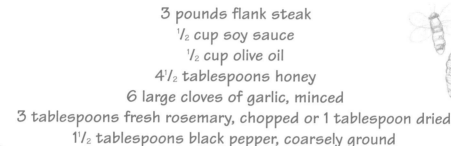

3 pounds flank steak
$\frac{1}{2}$ cup soy sauce
$\frac{1}{2}$ cup olive oil
$4\frac{1}{2}$ tablespoons honey
6 large cloves of garlic, minced
3 tablespoons fresh rosemary, chopped or 1 tablespoon dried
$1\frac{1}{2}$ tablespoons black pepper, coarsely ground
$1\frac{1}{2}$ teaspoons salt

Mix all of the ingredients, except the steak, in a heavy-duty plastic bag. Add steak and turn to coat. Seal tightly and refrigerate at least 2 hours. (Longer makes it better) Preheat the broiler, or prepare the grill. Remove steak from the bag; discard the marinade. Cook to desired doneness. Let rest 5-10 minutes; slice across the grain into thin strips and serve. Use the leftovers (if there are any) for salad topping!

Serves: 6

MEATS & MAIN DISHES

GRILLED FLANK STEAK

Flank steak is a terrific cut of beef. It's lean and quick-cooking. When you use this marinade, you get a hint of the soy, coupled with the tangy sweetness of the balsamic and sugar.

2 pounds flank steak
2 large shallots
9 tablespoons balsamic vinegar
6 tablespoons sugar
6 tablespoons low-sodium soy sauce
Salt and pepper to taste

Pat the steak dry; cut crosswise at a 45° angle into 2 equal pieces. Season steaks with salt and pepper and transfer to a resealable heavy-duty plastic bag. Chop the shallots and stir together with remaining ingredients. Pour marinade into the plastic bag. Add steaks and marinate in the refrigerator for at least 2 hours, but preferably overnight. Turn several times while marinating. Remove steaks from the bag and discard the marinade. Grill or broil to the doneness preferred. Let stand for 10 minutes before carving. Great with sautéed Portobello mushrooms, or other mushrooms.

Serves: 4 - 6

ITALIAN-STYLE BEEF TENDERLOIN

Truly, tenderloin is the very best cut of beef. A little goes a long way. The pepper and Italian seasoning make a nice rub for the beef while Parmesan adds a unique flavor at the end of the cooking process.

4 pounds beef tenderloin, well-trimmed
1 teaspoon dried Italian seasoning
½ teaspoon freshly cracked pepper
2 tablespoons freshly grated Parmesan cheese
Salt to taste
Roasted vegetables (see page 109)

Preheat the oven to 425° F. Combine the dried Italian seasoning and pepper evenly onto the surface of the beef. Place meat on a rack in a shallow roasting pan. DO NOT COVER. Roast for 45 - 50 minutes for medium-rare to medium doneness. Remove from the oven, then sprinkle the grated cheese over the top. Let rest for 15 minutes. Carve into ½ inch thick slices. Serve with oven roasted vegetables.

Serves: 8 – 10

MEATS & MAIN DISHES

APPLE-RAISIN PORK CHOPS

Apples and pork go together in my book. Apples and apple juice sweeten the pork. Raisins provide an unexpected touch.

4 6-ounce boneless pork chops
$\frac{1}{3}$ cup black or golden raisins
2 apples, peeled and cored
$\frac{1}{2}$ cup apple juice
Salt and pepper to taste

Preheat oven to 350° F. Brown the pork chops in a large heavy skillet. Season with salt and pepper. Transfer to a baking dish and top with raisins and apples. Pour over apple juice. Cover with foil and bake for 1 hour, or until tender.

Serves: 2 – 4

ROAST LOIN OF PORK
WITH
ROSEMARY AND GARLIC

Garlic coupled with the fragrance and slightly lemony flavor
of rosemary make this a dish to remember!

5 pound loin of pork, skin scored
1 large bunch of rosemary sprigs, about 8
5 cloves of garlic
$^3/_4$ cup dry white wine
4 bay leaves

Preheat the oven to 475° F. Place the rosemary branches and a few bay leaves in a baking dish large enough to hold the pork. Peel the garlic cloves and squash them to make a puree. Push the pureed garlic into the scores in the pork fat. Rub pork with salt and fresh pepper and top with a rosemary sprig.

Arrange pork, fat side up. Cook for 20 minutes. Then lower the temperature to 375° F. Add half the wine to the pan and cook for $1^1/_2$ hours more. Baste every 20 minutes. Add more wine, if necessary, to leave a thin layer of liquid in the bottom of the pan throughout the cooking time. (Meat is cooked when the juices run clear after sticking with a fork.) Remove from oven and place pork on a platter. Cover with foil to keep warm. Discard rosemary and bay leaves from pan and any fat. Place pan over moderate heat. When it bubbles, add 3 or 4 tablespoons water. Scrape bits at the bottom; bring to boil and simmer 2 minutes. (Careful it doesn't burn.)
Strain the juices and serve with the meat.

Serves: 8 – 10

GRILLED HOISIN-MARINATED PORK

Hoisin sauce is dark, sweet and spicy. Experiment and you'll find yourself using it again and again. When you add the other ingredients for this dish, you get a robust Asian sauce.

2 pounds pork tenderloin
¼ cup hoisin sauce
2 tablespoons rice wine vinegar
2 tablespoons low-sodium soy sauce
3 cloves garlic, coarsely chopped
1 teaspoon sesame oil
Salt and freshly ground pepper

Combine hoisin, vinegar, soy sauce, garlic and sesame oil in a large non-metallic bowl. Marinate the tenderloin in this mixture 3-4 hours, or overnight, turning once or twice. Preheat the broiler or grill. Remove pork from the marinade, removing any excess. Season with salt and pepper. Grill for 10-12 minutes, or until done.

Serves: 4

PORK TENDERLOIN
WITH
MUSTARD SAUCE

When I have a pork tenderloin and I just can't think of what to do with it, invariably I remember this recipe. The mustard blends with the other ingredients to make a very savory sauce.

1-2 pounds tenderloin of pork
2 tablespoons coarse mustard, such as tarragon or pommery
1 tablespoon vegetable oil
½ cup vermouth, or dry white wine
1 tablespoon all-purpose flour
1 tablespoon butter, softened and unsalted

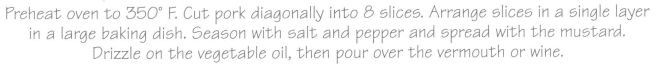

Preheat oven to 350° F. Cut pork diagonally into 8 slices. Arrange slices in a single layer in a large baking dish. Season with salt and pepper and spread with the mustard. Drizzle on the vegetable oil, then pour over the vermouth or wine.

Cover the dish tightly with foil. Bake, basting twice, for 30 – 40 minutes. Remove from the oven and take slices of pork out onto a plate (cover to keep warm). Meanwhile, blend together the butter and flour to make a roux. Add this mixture to the liquid in the dish and cook over moderately high heat, whisking constantly, for 1 minute or until thickened. Spoon over the pork.

Serves: 2 – 4

MEATS & MAIN DISHES

SESAME-GARLIC GRILLED PORK TENDERLOIN

This tenderloin is always a hit with guests. Use chicken for another variation.
Be sure to use a good sherry and fresh, fresh, garlic.

1¹/₂ pounds pork tenderloin
4 tablespoons soy sauce
2 tablespoons sesame oil
2 tablespoons brown sugar
¹/₂ teaspoon honey
1 tablespoon dry sherry
4 cloves garlic, minced
2 tablespoons sesame seeds, toasted
3-4 scallions, sliced diagonally

Combine soy, sesame oil, brown sugar, honey, sherry, garlic, sesame seeds and scallions for the marinade. Mix well. Marinate pork, covered, overnight in the refrigerator. Remove pork from the marinade, discard. Grill or broil pork, turning occasionally, 15-20 minutes. Let rest 5 minutes, then carve into medallions.

Serves: 4

HERBED APRICOT PORK TENDERLOIN

Apricot preserves add sweetness. Lots of herbs add dash.
Very low in calories and fat. Healthy and good!!!

2 1 pound pork tenderloins, fat trimmed
1 teaspoon dried thyme
1 teaspoon dried sage
1 teaspoon ground cinnamon
$\frac{1}{4}$ teaspoon garlic powder
$\frac{1}{4}$ teaspoon salt
$\frac{1}{4}$ cup apricot preserves
Cooking spray

Preheat oven to 425° F. Combine herbs, spices and salt in a shallow dish. Brush the pork with the preserves. Roll each tenderloin in the herb and spice mixture and place on a broiler pan coated with cooking spray. Bake for about 30 minutes. Check for doneness, then cover and let stand 10 minutes before slicing.

Serves: 8

MEATS & MAIN DISHES

PORK, CASHEW & GREEN BEAN STIR-FRY

Whenever I make this entree, I think I'm in my own Chinese restaurant. The garlic,
ginger and sesame oil create Asian-induced cravings. Cashews add crunch and a little saltiness.
This dish is low in calories and low in fat.

1 pound pork tenderloin, cut into ¼ inch thick slices
¼ cup low-sodium soy sauce
2 teaspoons cornstarch
4 cups fresh cut green beans (about 1 lb.)
2 teaspoons dark sesame oil
Cooking spray
1 - 2 tablespoons fresh ginger, peeled and minced
2 garlic cloves, minced
¼ cup fat-free, low-sodium chicken broth
2 cups hot cooked rice
¼ cup cashews, chopped, unsalted and toasted

Combine the soy sauce and cornstarch in a medium-size bowl, and add the pork, stirring to coat. Cover and chill. Cook the green beans in boiling water for 5 minutes and drain. Plunge in ice water to stop the cooking and drain again. Heat sesame oil in a large skillet coated with cooking spray over medium-high heat. Add the ginger and the garlic and sauté for 1 minute. Add the pork mixture and stir-fry for 2 minutes. Next stir in green beans and stir-fry for 2 minutes, or until pork is done. Add broth, reduce heat and simmer 2 minutes. Serve over the hot rice and sprinkle with the cashews.

Serves: 4

ASIAN-STYLE MARINATED PORK STRIPS

Most of my favorite pork recipes use soy, garlic and ginger.
They always work together. Sesame seeds are a delightful crunchy, nutty addition.

2 pork tenderloins, trimmed of fat and split lengthwise
$\frac{1}{2}$ cup soy sauce
3 tablespoons onions, minced
2 cloves garlic, minced
2 teaspoons ground ginger
$\frac{1}{4}$ cup sesame seeds
2 tablespoons vegetable oil

Preheat oven to 350° F. Combine all ingredients, except pork and oil, in a small bowl. Place pork in heavy-duty resealable bag and pour mixture over. Marinate for 3 hours in the refrigerator, turning several times to make sure pork is coated. Remove from bag; dry lightly in paper towels. Coat pork with oil and sauté in a skillet until seared. Finish in oven or on the grill. Don't let it overcook.

Serves: 4

RACK OF LAMB
WITH
FRESH ROSEMARY

When you combine Dijon mustard with rosemary and lamb, you have created one of the best culinary creations ever. The natural flavor and tenderness of the lamb and a beautiful presentation to your guests will make for many "oohs" and "aahs!"

2 racks of lamb, trimmed with about 7 ribs each
with 2 inches of bone exposed
2 tablespoons Dijon mustard
1 tablespoon fresh rosemary leaves, finely chopped
2 tablespoons fresh squeezed lemon juice
4 tablespoons extra virgin olive oil
Salt and freshly ground pepper to taste

Preheat oven to 500° F. In a small bowl, combine mustard, rosemary, lemon juice and olive oil. On the fat side of the racks, make shallow crisscross marks with a sharp knife. Fold a double strip of foil over the rib ends to keep them from burning. Brush the mustard-rosemary mixture over the tops and sides of the racks. Place racks rib - end down in a roasting pan. Season with salt and pepper. Roast in the center of the oven about 10 minutes, until the lamb is well-seared. Reduce heat to 400° F. and roast 20-30 minutes more (you may have to cut into center to check for doneness.) Remove from oven and let stand covered loosely with foil about 15 minutes. Carve into individual ribs and serve.

Serves: 4 – 6

FRESH HERBED LEG OF LAMB

The leg always is heartier than the chops. By marinating overnight the flavors of the garlic, rosemary and vinegar meld.

5 - 6 pound leg of lamb
$\frac{1}{4}$ cup extra virgin olive oil
1 large clove garlic, cut into slivers
$\frac{1}{4}$ cup wine vinegar
1 tablespoon fresh chopped rosemary
Salt and freshly ground pepper

Season lamb with salt and pepper. Make slits in the lamb and insert slivers of garlic. Place leg of lamb in a heavy-duty resealable plastic bag. Mix remaining ingredients; pour over lamb. Marinate in the refrigerator overnight, turning occasionally.
To cook, place on a rack and roast in a preheated 325° F. oven for 2 - 2 $\frac{1}{2}$ hours.
Let racks rest 15 minutes before carving.

Serves: 6 – 8

VEAL CHOPS
WITH
BALSAMIC VINEGAR & VERMOUTH

Veal chops are more robust than scallopini and make a hearty meal. Balsamic vinegar is sweet and pungent; it raises the level of flavor in the chops from usual to unusually delicious!

6 6-ounce veal chops
3 garlic cloves, minced
2 tablespoons chopped fresh rosemary or 2 teaspoons dried
2 tablespoons chopped fresh thyme or 2 teaspoons dried
2 tablespoons extra virgin olive oil
3/4 cup balsamic vinegar
1 tablespoon vermouth
Additional chopped fresh thyme

Place the veal chops in a glass baking dish. Rub both sides with garlic, rosemary and thyme. Cover and refrigerate for several hours or even 1 day ahead. Preheat oven to 450° F. Carefully heat 1 tablespoon olive oil in each of 2 heavy ovenproof skillets over high heat. Season veal with salt and pepper. Add 3 chops to each skillet; sear until brown, about 3 minutes per side.

Transfer skillets to the oven and roast chops for about 8 minutes. Carefully remove chops from the oven and onto a platter. Add the vinegar to 1 skillet; bring to a boil, scraping up the brown bits. Pour mixture into the second skillet. Add the vermouth and boil until a syrupy consistency, stirring occasionally to loosen brown bits, about 3 minutes. Pour over veal. Sprinkle with additional chopped thyme.

Serves: 6

VEAL CUTLETS
WITH
BASIL

Don't be afraid to try veal. It has a more delicate flavor than beef, is very tender and cooks quickly. Basil and a good white wine add seasoning and polish. Good with either rice or pasta.

3 tablespoons extra virgin olive oil
2 large cloves garlic, chopped
8 2-ounce veal cutlets (scaloppine)
All-purpose flour
1 cup dry white wine
$\frac{1}{2}$ cup packed whole basil leaves
Thinly sliced fresh basil

Heat the oil in a skillet over medium heat. Add the garlic and sauté 1 minute. Season veal with salt and pepper and dust with flour. Add veal to the pan and cook 1 minute per side. Transfer the meat to a plate and cover with foil to keep warm. Add wine and whole basil leaves. Simmer 5 minutes.

Return the veal to the pan and heat through. Using a slotted spoon, transfer the veal to plates. Boil the remaining liquid until it reduces, about 3 minutes. Spoon over the veal cutlets and garnish with sliced basil.

Serves: 4

MEATS & MAIN DISHES

NOTES

Vegetables

EASY EGGPLANT PARMIGIANA

I love the combination of eggplant and the sweet and spicy flavor of a good jarred spaghetti sauce topped with mozzarella that melts over the whole concoction. In very short order a little bit of Italy can be on your table.

1 medium-size unpeeled eggplant, cut into ½ inch slices
¼ cup olive or vegetable oil
1 cup spaghetti sauce
1 tablespoon grated onion
1 clove garlic, minced
½ tablespoon salt
½ tablespoon fresh cracked pepper
⅓ cup Parmesan cheese
4 ounces mozzarella cheese, sliced and cut into thin strips

Place eggplant slices on a greased broiler pan. Brush with some of the oil, preferably olive oil. Broil 4-5 inches from the heat for about 5 minutes. Turn and brush with remaining oil. Broil for 4 minutes more. Combine spaghetti sauce, onion, garlic and salt. Spread each slice with some of the mixture and sprinkle with Parmesan. Top each slice with 3 thin strips of mozzarella. Broil 1-2 minutes more, or until lightly brown and cheese melts.

Serves: 4

YELLOW SQUASH CASSEROLE

This is a down-home comfort food recipe that my kids loved from the time they could eat table food. The squash becomes soft and creamy, the consistency is almost soufflé-like, and the cheese just melts over the top and makes it all so yummy.

4 medium-size yellow squash
2 tablespoons butter
1½ cups low-fat or skim milk (approximately)
2 cups dry bread crumbs (approximately)
Salt and pepper to taste
4 slices of American cheese

Preheat oven to 350° F. Melt butter in a square baking dish. Cut squash into ½ inch wide rounds and place into baking dish with the butter. Pour over milk to cover squash. Then add enough bread crumbs to almost absorb all the milk. Season with salt and pepper and top with the cheese slices.

Cover with foil and bake for 30 to 40 minutes or until tender. Uncover baking dish and finish cooking until cheese melts and begins to brown.

Serves: 4

BAKED VIDALIA ONIONS

Vidalia's are a special sweet treat; they get tender and even sweeter when cooked.
The Parmesan adds a touch that goes well with these so highly revered bulbs.
These are also good as an appetizer; like a "blossom" without the fat.

4 large Vidalia onions
2 – 3 tablespoons butter, cut into small pieces
1 teaspoon salt
$\frac{1}{4}$ teaspoon pepper
1 cup Parmesan cheese, shredded (or whatever cheese you like)

Preheat oven to 400° F. Peel onions, leaving root ends intact. Cut each onion from top to bottom into 8ths, cutting to, but not through, the root ends. Place each onion on a lightly greased 12-inch square of foil. Press the butter evenly into each of the cuts in the onions. Sprinkle with salt and pepper; then top with cheese.

Wrap up in the foil and arrange in a baking pan. Bake for 1 hour.

Serves: 4

BROILED HERBED EGGPLANT

Choose an eggplant that is firm with smooth skin. Use it right away; it gets bitter as it ages. Once you develop an (acquired) taste for this wonderful vegetable, you'll want to try it a hundred different ways.

1 large firm eggplant, cut into rounds
1/4 cup extra virgin olive oil
1/8 teaspoon dried basil
1/8 teaspoon dried thyme
1/8 teaspoon dried oregano
1 teaspoon salt
1/2 teaspoon fresh ground pepper
1 teaspoon finely minced garlic
2 tablespoons extra virgin olive oil
2 tablespoons butter
1 tablespoon chopped, fresh parsley
1/4 cup dried breadcrumbs

In a small pan, mix 1/4 cup olive oil, basil, thyme, oregano, teaspoon salt, pepper and minced garlic. Cut eggplant horizontally into 8 round slices, then brush both sides with the olive oil mixture. Lay the slices on a baking sheet; bake 15 minutes in a preheated 375° F. oven. Turn each slice and bake 15 minutes more. Meanwhile, melt 2 tablespoons butter in the same pan that the olive oil mixture was in; stir in the bread crumbs. Spoon this mixture over the eggplant slices; broil until brown, 2-3 minutes. Watch carefully.

Serves: 4

ROASTED ZUCCHINI

Fresh herbs roasted with zucchini give the palate a clean, fresh taste.
This squash is nearly always a very good buy.

4 medium-size zucchini
¼ cup extra virgin olive oil
2 tablespoons lemon juice
Fresh herbs
Salt and pepper to taste

Preheat oven to 375° F. Cut medium-size zucchini into 1-inch lengths. Toss lightly with olive oil, salt and pepper and fresh herbs of your choice. Roast for about 40 minutes, or until tender. Sprinkle with lemon juice before serving.

Serves: 4 – 6

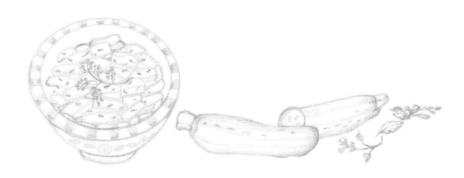

GARLIC ROASTED VEGETABLES

When you pair basic roasted vegetables with lots of creamy, nutty, roasted garlic you get a marvelous marriage. Tossed with grated Parmesan, it then becomes a veritable feast. Works well with roasts, chops and chicken.

1 large whole bulb garlic
3 medium baking potatoes or Yukon Golds, quartered
4 small onions, peeled and halved lengthwise
6 small plum tomatoes, halved lengthwise
2 medium zucchini, cut into $3/4$ inch slices
2 tablespoons extra virgin olive oil
1 teaspoon dried Italian seasoning
$1/2$ teaspoon pepper
$1/4$ cup grated Parmesan cheese
1 teaspoon salt

Preheat oven to 425° F. Cut $3/4$ inch off the top of the unpeeled garlic bulb, cutting through the tip of each clove and discard. Wrap garlic securely in foil; set aside. In a large bowl, combine olive oil, Italian seasoning, salt and pepper. Add vegetables and toss to coat. Set aside tomatoes and zucchini in a separate bowl. Arrange potatoes, onions and foil wrapped garlic on a jelly roll pan, or shallow baking dish, then roast for about 30 minutes. Add tomatoes and zucchini. Continue to roast 15-20 minutes more or until all vegetables are tender and lightly browned. Remove vegetables to a large bowl; unwrap garlic and squeeze softened cloves over the vegetables. Toss with Parmesan and additional salt and pepper if desired.

Serves: 8 – 10

BALSAMIC ROASTED ASPARAGUS

Asparagus is my favorite vegetable and this is my favorite cooking method. The balsamic provides a tangy sweet flavor to the slightly smoky-flavored roasted asparagus. I like to top it off with shaved Parmesan. Great served warm, or at room temperature.

1 bunch of asparagus, medium thickness
$\frac{1}{4}$ cup extra virgin olive oil
2 tablespoons balsamic vinegar
Salt and pepper to taste
Fresh shaved Parmesan (optional)

Preheat oven to 450° F. Wash and stem asparagus and dry well. Line up on a parchment or foil-lined baking sheet. Drizzle with a little olive oil. Bake until slightly brown at the tips, about 10 minutes. Remove from baking sheet; place on platter and drizzle with a little balsamic vinegar. Season with salt and freshly ground pepper.

Serves: 4

ROASTED GARLIC

Garlic has to be one of nature's finest creations. It becomes creamy and nutty when you roasted. This culinary delight is great on breads, meats, fish, chicken, even pizza. (Use the earlier method of wrapping the garlic heads in foil before roasting, if you prefer.)

4 heads of garlic
½ cup olive oil
1 sprig fresh thyme
3 tablespoons fresh lemon juice

Preheat oven to 400° F. Place whole, firm, unpeeled heads of garlic in a shallow baking dish. Drizzle with a little olive oil, then sprinkle with salt and pepper. Bake for 1 hour. Cool. Extract the softened garlic from the cloves into a small sterilized jar. Add a sprig of fresh thyme and the juice of ½ of a fresh lemon. Top with olive oil just to cover. Cover and refrigerate for up to 10 days.

Makes: About 1 cup

HEAVENLY ROASTED TOMATOES

The essence of tomato comes out when it's roasted. The uses are endless.
These tomatoes are always in my refrigerator.

8 large ripe plum tomatoes
3 tablespoons kosher salt
3 tablespoons freshly ground pepper
1/4 cup granulated sugar
2 tablespoons extra virgin olive oil
1/2 - 3/4 cup fresh herbs

Preheat oven to 250° F. Slice tomatoes thickly, 3-4 slices per tomato (use ends for something else). Place slices on a parchment-lined baking sheet. Mix salt, pepper and sugar together. Brush tomatoes with olive oil; then sprinkle each slice with large pinch o sugar mixture and herbs. Roast for 2-3 hours, until tender but not dried out. They will keep in the refrigerator in a closed container for a week or a little more. Reduce or omit the sugar if you like.

Serve: 4 - 6

STIR-FRIED SUGAR SNAP PEAS
&
CHERRY TOMATOES

Simple and very attractive on the plate! Use cherry bells for great results.
Pair with meat, poultry or fish.

2 tablespoons extra virgin olive oil
12 ounces sugar snap peas, stems and strings removed
20 small cherry tomatoes (washed, dried and stemmed)
2 large shallots, peeled and thinly sliced
2 teaspoons white wine vinegar

Heat oil in a heavy medium skillet over medium-high heat. Add peas, tomatoes and shallots. Stir-fry until peas are bright green and tomatoes are heated through, about 3 minutes. Sprinkle with vinegar and toss to coat. Season with salt and pepper and serve.

Serves : 4

APPLE MALLOW YAMBAKE

This is a dish loved by kids, but adults will also enjoy. It's a great way to get the kids to eat their veggies. I served this one to the Freedman children when they were quite young, so it's been around a long time.

2 apples, peeled and sliced
$1/2$ cup brown sugar
$1/2$ teaspoon cinnamon
2 17-ounce can yams, drained
2 - 3 tablespoons butter
2 cups miniature marshmallows

Preheat oven to 350°F. Toss apples with brown sugar and cinnamon. Alternate layers of apples and yams in a lightly buttered 1½ quart baking dish. Dot with butter. Cover and bake 35 – 40 minutes. Top with marshmallows and broil until lightly browned.

Makes: 6 – 8 servings

SWEET POTATO-APPLE BAKE

This "bake" is low in calories and fat and fun for kids, too.
Sweet poatoes and apples provide great nutrition. Don't tell the kids.

6 cups thinly sliced peeled sweet potatoes (about 2 lbs.)
3 cups peeled and sliced Granny Smith apples
$\frac{1}{2}$ teaspoon salt, divided
Cooking spray
3 tablespoons maple syrup (the real stuff)
2 tablespoons butter, melted

Coat a 10-inch square casserole with cooking spray. Arrange 3 cups sweet potato and 1$\frac{1}{2}$ cups apple in casserole; sprinkle with $\frac{1}{4}$ teaspoon salt. Combine syrup and butter; stir well. Drizzle half of syrup mixture over the potatoes. Repeat procedure with remaining ingredients. Cover with plastic wrap. MICROWAVE on high 10 minutes, rotating half-turn after 5 minutes. Let stand, covered, about 5 minutes.

Serves: 6 – 8

OVEN FRIED POTATOES

French fries without the frying. These are even better because they puff up when baked and they're smothered with the delicious flavors of garlic and Parmesan. They are a sure hit with young ones. Again, less fat – better for you.

8 large unpeeled baking potatoes, each cut into 8 wedges
$1/3$ cup extra virgin olive oil
2 tablespoons Parmesan cheese
1 teaspoon salt
$1/2$ teaspoon garlic powder
$1/2$ teaspoon paprika
$1/4$ teaspoon freshly ground pepper

Preheat oven to 375° F. Arrange potato wedges, peel side down, in 2 shallow baking pans. Mix all remaining ingredients in a bowl and brush over the potato wedges.

Bake for 45 minutes until golden brown and tender, brushing occasionally with oil mixture. Serve immediately.

Serves: 8

POTATOES BOULANGERIE

I've had this recipe for ages and have no idea why it has this name.
But it's a really good side dish and that's all that matters.

3 large potatoes, Yukon Gold preferably
1 large onion, sliced
1 teaspoon fresh parsley
2 tablespoons unsalted butter
¼ cup boiling water
Salt and pepper to taste

Preheat the oven to 400° F. Peel and slice potatoes. In a large bowl combine potatoes with 1 small onion, sliced. Add chopped parsley and salt and pepper to your taste.

Lightly butter a shallow baking dish and spread potato-onion mixture about ½ inch deep. Dot with 2 tablespoons butter and add boiling water. Bake for 30-40 minutes or until brown and crusty on the top. All water should be absorbed.

Serves: 4, depending on size of potatoes

NEW POTATOES & FRESH GREEN BEANS

Another good marriage. Tarragon gives a slight anise flavor. Serve this dish hot, cold, or at room temperature with meat, poultry, or fish. I like the crunch of the green beans and the slight crispiness of the potatoes. Other fresh chopped herbs work. Experiment to find your favorite.

1½ pounds fresh green beans, blanched
1 pound new potatoes, quartered
2 tablespoons olive oil
1 tablespoon fresh tarragon, chopped
1 tablespoon fresh ground pepper
¼ cup vinaigrette dressing (homemade or bottled)
Cooking spray

Preheat oven to 350° F. Toss all of the ingredients together and pour into a 3-quart casserole dish coated with cooking spray. Bake for 50 - 60 minutes, stirring twice during cooking time. Toss with vinaigrette dressing just before serving.

Serves: 4 – 6

ROSEMARY ROASTED POTATOES

Rosemary and these "crunchy"potatoes naturally go together. Fresh herbs makes it even better. Low calorie and virtually no fat.

3 large baking potatoes, unpeeled
Olive oil flavored cooking spray
$1/4$ teaspoon salt
$1^1/_2$ teaspoon dried rosemary or 3 teaspoons fresh rosemary
$1/2$ teaspoon freshly ground pepper

Preheat oven to 375° F. Wash potatoes, pat dry, then cut into $1/4$ inch slices. Coat baking sheet with cooking spray. Arrange slices into 4 rows on a baking sheet, overlapping half of each slice with the next, forming 4 rounds. Sprinkle with salt, then combine rosemary and pepper. Sprinkle potatoes with half the mixture; set aside the remaining mixture. Bake for 20 minutes, then turn, coat with cooking spray and sprinkle with remaining rosemary mixture. Bake an additional 20 minutes.
Remove with a spatula and serve.

Serves: 4

VEGETABLES

MOM'S KUGEL

This is a traditional Jewish noodle pudding which my children have always loved. No two kugel recipes are alike; every recipe has a special uniqueness. My mother always made this sweet version that I've described, but there are countless variations. It is always served as a side dish like a vegetable. This variation freezes well and will keep up to six weeks frozen.

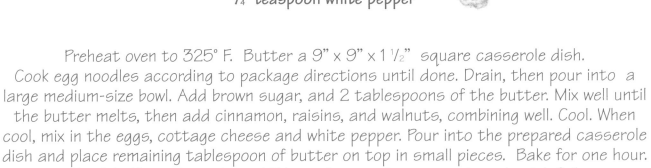

1 8-ounce package egg noodles
2 tablespoons brown sugar, firmly packed
3 tablespoons butter
1 teaspoon cinnamon, ground
$1/4$ cup brown raisins
$1/4$ cup walnuts, chopped
2 eggs, well beaten
4 tablespoons cottage cheese
$1/4$ teaspoon white pepper

Preheat oven to 325° F. Butter a 9" x 9" x 1 $1/2$" square casserole dish.
Cook egg noodles according to package directions until done. Drain, then pour into a large medium-size bowl. Add brown sugar, and 2 tablespoons of the butter. Mix well until the butter melts, then add cinnamon, raisins, and walnuts, combining well. Cool. When cool, mix in the eggs, cottage cheese and white pepper. Pour into the prepared casserole dish and place remaining tablespoon of butter on top in small pieces. Bake for one hour. Check halfway through, and if browning too fast, cover loosely with foil.
Uncover for the last 10 - 15 minutes.

Serves: 6 - 8

Pasta & Rice

RITA'S YELLOW RICE

Saffron, the most expensive spice in the world, makes a simple rice become a star. Golden colored rice studded with bits of the red tomato is simply lovely with baked chicken, or a well-seared slice of beef. Yellow rice is a classic Spanish dish in the homes of thousands of Tampa residents. In Tampa we were raised on it! Omit the meat, or seafood, if you are a vegetarian, or if you prefer a simpler side dish. Whatever you choose, this dish says "Tampa."

6 ounces cooked pork, diced (or cooked shrimp or chicken)
1 cup Uncle Ben's converted white rice®
1 large onion, chopped
2 cloves garlic, minced
1 tomato, seeded and diced
2 tablespoons extra virgin olive oil
2$\frac{1}{2}$ cups boiling water
Few threads of saffon or 2 teaspoons of Bijol®
1 bay leaf, whole
$\frac{1}{8}$ teaspoon paprika
2 teaspoons thinly sliced pimiento for granish
$\frac{1}{4}$ cup frozen peas for garnish

Add olive oil to a medium-size sauté pan. When heated, add in onion, garlic and tomato and cook for about 1 minute. Add rice and stir until it mixture is coated with the oil. Pour rice into boiling water, then add saffron, bay leaf and paprika. Stir well. Cover and cook on low heat until almost all of the water is absorbed, about 20 minutes. Add pork (or chicken or seafood) and mix well. Allow to cook for a few minutes, then remove from the heat. Remove the bay leaf and discard. Garnish with peas and pimiento just before serving.

Serves: 4

OVEN-BAKED RICE PILAF

When you remove the cover from this side dish, watch out for the steam! Not only is it a comfort food, but it is great for a crowd and it's also an easy do-ahead dish for busy moms.

1 tablespoon unsalted butter
1 cup Uncle Ben's® Converted Rice
2$\frac{1}{2}$ cups water
2 tablespoons toasted pine nuts
$\frac{1}{2}$ cup sautéed mushrooms
$\frac{1}{2}$ cup sautéed onions
Salt to taste

Preheat oven to 350° F. Melt butter in a medium-size baking dish, then add rice and stir well to coat the kernels. Add salt and water, then cover and bake for about 55 minutes, or until water is absorbed. Add the toasted pine nuts, sautéed mushrooms, sautéed onions, salt and any other ingredients that may appeal to you.

Serves: 4

PASTA & RICE

PENNE AU GRATIN

When you want to "go over the top," whip up this pasta and cheese dish. Serve it as a gourmet special or as comfort food for the entire family. It's rich and creamy, with just a hint of tomato. It tastes like homemade macaroni and cheese with a little spice to it.

6 ounces penne pasta
1$\frac{1}{2}$ teaspoons unsalted butter
1 tablespoon extra virgin olive oil
2 tablespoons all - purpose flour
2$\frac{1}{2}$ cups milk (for lower fat, skim is ok)
4$\frac{1}{2}$-ounces cheddar cheese, cut into $\frac{1}{2}$ inch cubes (reduced fat cheddar works)
$\frac{3}{4}$ teaspoon salt
$\frac{3}{4}$ teaspoon freshly ground pepper
1 large tomato, seeded and cut into $\frac{1}{2}$ inch cubes
1$\frac{1}{2}$ tablespoons freshly grated Parmesan cheese
$\frac{1}{2}$ teaspoon paprika

Preheat oven to 400° F. Cook pasta for about 8 minutes, until just done. Drain and rinse under cold water, until cool, then set aside. Combine butter and oil in a saucepan, then carefully whisk in the flour. Cook the mixture over medium heat for about 10 seconds being careful not to scorch. Add the milk; stir. Quickly bring the mixture to a boil for about 10 seconds. Add the cheddar cheese, salt and pepper and mix well. Cook over low heat for 3-4 minutes and set aside. Mix the pasta with the sauce and transfer to a lightly-buttered shallow baking dish. Top with the tomato and sprinkle with Parmesan and paprika. Bake for about 30 minutes, or until bubbly and nicely browned. Serve immediately.

Serves: 4

FUSILLI
WITH
CHEVRE, TOMATOES & BASIL

The slight tartness of the chevre (goat cheese) mixed with the tanginess of the basil and tomatoes creates a mélange of flavors. As the chevre melts into the hot pasta, it becomes oh, so creamy! Use the Greek version of chevre; called feta for an excellent variation.

1$\frac{1}{2}$ pounds plum tomatoes
$\frac{1}{4}$ cup extra virgin olive oil
2 teaspoons red wine vinegar
1 large garlic clove, minced
1 pound fusilli (spiral) pasta
3 - 4 ounces soft fresh goat cheese, such as Montrachet (or feta), cut into small pieces
$\frac{1}{3}$ cup thinly sliced fresh basil

Peel, seed and chop the tomatoes. Place in a large non-metallic bowl and mix in the olive oil, vinegar and garlic. Season to taste with salt and pepper. Cook the pasta until just tender but still firm; drain. Add pasta, chevre cheese and basil to the tomato mixture. Toss until well blended and the cheese melts. Season to taste with salt and pepper.

Serves: 4

PASTA & RICE

PASTA
WITH
UNCOOKED TOMATO SAUCE

Summer in a pasta! The classic tomato, basil, mozzarella trio enlivened with the garlic, oil and vinegar creating a mouth-watering version that few are able to resist. This is a perfect summertime dish and good the next day as a cold salad.

1 pound dried pasta, preferably angel's hair
1 1/2 pounds plum tomatoes, seeded and chopped
3 garlic cloves, minced
1/2 cup packed fresh basil leaves, chopped roughly
1 cup diced mozzarella
1/2 cup extra virgin olive oil
2 tablespoons red wine vinegar
Salt and pepper

In a large non-metallic mixing bowl combine all ingredients except pasta. Let stand, covered, at room temperature, for about 2 hours. Just before serving, cook pasta; drain and toss with the sauce.

Serves: 4 - 6

ROASTED GARLIC ORZO

n Italian, the word "orzo" means "barley," but in actuality it's a tiny rice-shaped pasta. Roasted garlic has a nutty taste and creamy texture. The poppy seeds make it crunchy; the parsley adds a clean note. Mixed together with the pasta, these few ingredients produce a complex creation.

6 large garlic cloves, unpeeled
2 tablespoon unsalted butter
4 tablespoons fresh parsley, chopped
2 teaspoons poppy seeds
1 cup orzo* pasta

Preheat oven to 450° F. Wrap garlic cloves tightly in foil and roast 25 minutes until tender. While garlic is roasting, dry-toast poppy seeds over moderate heat in a sauté pan (watch carefully so they don't burn). Cool slightly. Remove garlic from foil, extract garlic by squeezing, then mash to a paste. Add in roasted poppy seeds, butter and parsley into the garlic mixture.

Cook orzo pasta according to package directions, until just done; drain and reserve ¼ cup of the cooking water. Mix orzo pasta, half of the reserved water and the garlic mixture. Combine well, season with salt and pepper to taste. Add more reserved water if necessary. Serve immediately.

*Available at most supermarkets.

Serves: 4

PASTA & RICE

NOTES

Desserts, Cookies & Sweets

APPLE ROSIE

This classic cobbler is fragrant with the aromas of cinnamon, lemon and apple. When combined, they become a treat that is pure "comfort food," yet luscious enough to serve to an elegant dinner party.

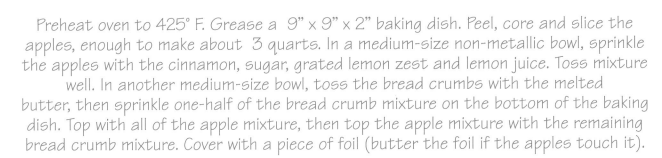

12 Granny Smith apples
3/4 teaspoon cinnamon or more, depending on your liking
1/2 cup granulated sugar
1 teaspoon grated lemon zest
1/4 cup lemon juice
2 cups fresh bread crumbs
1/2 cup melted butter
1 quart vanilla ice cream

Preheat oven to 425° F. Grease a 9" x 9" x 2" baking dish. Peel, core and slice the apples, enough to make about 3 quarts. In a medium-size non-metallic bowl, sprinkle the apples with the cinnamon, sugar, grated lemon zest and lemon juice. Toss mixture well. In another medium-size bowl, toss the bread crumbs with the melted butter, then sprinkle one-half of the bread crumb mixture on the bottom of the baking dish. Top with all of the apple mixture, then top the apple mixture with the remaining bread crumb mixture. Cover with a piece of foil (butter the foil if the apples touch it).

Bake for 30 minutes, then remove the foil and bake another 30 minutes uncovered. Remove from oven, cook and serve warm or at room temperature. Serve with a dollop of cinnamon-laced whipped cream, or a scoop of vanilla ice cream.

Serves: 4 – 6

BLUEBERRY PEACH CRISP

I truly love fresh fruit and try to purchase those in season to ensure the best quality and value. Here's a healthful – though not totally calorie-free – dessert. Needless to say, adding a few scoops of vanilla ice cream to each plate enhances the feast!

1 cup all-purpose flour
$^3/_4$ cups granulated sugar
1 teaspoons baking powder
$^1/_2$ teaspoons salt
1 unbeaten egg
2 cups rinsed and dried fresh blueberries
3 cups peeled and sliced fresh peaches
3 tablespoons sugar
$^1/_2$ teaspoons cinnamon, or to taste
$^1/_4$ cup melted unsalted butter

Preheat oven to 375° F. Grease an 8" x 8" x 2" baking dish. Combine the flour, sugar, baking powder and salt in a medium bowl. Stir in the unbeaten egg and mix with a fork until crumbly. Place the blueberries and peaches in buttered baking dish. Mix the sugar with the cinnamon, then pour over the fruit mixture. Drizzle with melted butter. Bake for 35 - 40 minutes, or until the top is well-browned.

Serves: 6

CINNAMON PEACH COBBLER

A crumbly topping adds a lovely contrast to the pungency of the fresh citrus.
No need to peel the peaches.

5 cups sliced unpeeled fresh peaches
Vegetable oil spray
1½ tablespoons fresh lemon juice
1 cup all-purpose flour
1 cup granulated sugar
½ teaspoon salt
1 egg, beaten
6 tablespoons melted butter
Whipped cream or ice cream
Cinnamon

Preheat oven to 375° F. Coat an 8" x 8" x 1 ½" square baking pan, or dish, with vegetable spray. Sprinkle peaches with lemon juice and toss to coat. Spread mixture evenly into the baking pan. Mix together flour, sugar and salt. Add the egg, then toss with a fork until crumbly. Sprinkle mixture over the peaches, then drizzle with the melted butter. Place in preheated oven for about 45 minutes, or until golden brown. Serve warm with whipped cream or vanilla ice cream and pass the cinnamon.

Serves: 4 – 6

CHOCOLATE CHIP WHIP

My kids absolutely loved this "mush," their favorite name for this yummy treat which they made with little help from mom. You can substitute just about any kind of cookie, but we used our favorite. It's still their favorite.

1 12-ounce package Chips Ahoy® Chocolate chip cookies
1¹/₂ cups whole milk
1 8-ounce container of Cool Whip® whipped topping

Dip cookies one at a time into the milk, then place them in a shallow dish or pie plate, side by side, in a circular fashion. Using a wide spatula, spread the topping over the cookies as evenly as possible. Repeat a second and then a third time, ending with the whipped topping. Refrigerate your creation overnight, covered.
Cut into triangles to serve.

Serves: 4 – 6

DESSERTS, COOKIES & SWEETS

CHOCOLATE CHIP CAKE

This cake freezes well, but be sure to leave out the powdered sugar, then to dust it on after thawing. It's a quick dessert and oh, so easy. Duncan Hines is the only kind we use, but feel free to use your favorite.

1 18¼-ounce package Duncan Hines Devil's Food Cake Mix®
¼ cup vegetable oil
2 eggs
¼ cup water
1 3-ounce package Jello® instant chocolate pudding
1 cup chocolate chips
Confectioners' sugar for sprinkling on top

Preheat the oven to 350° F. Pour the vegetable oil into a 13" x 9" x 2" baking pan and tilt to make sure the bottom is completely covered. Place all the remaining ingredients into the pan and stir for about 2 minutes, or until very well blended. Bake for 35-45 minutes or until a tester comes out clean (make certain the top doesn't burn). Cool completely, then sprinkle the top with confectioners' sugar.

Serves: 16 - 20

MAPLE-CINNAMON BREAD PUDDING

This bread pudding has fewer calories than you might think, not to mention the lovely aroma. I use skim milk, but you can use whole milk and it will be even more delicious. Use freshly ground nutmeg for best results.

6 ounces Italian bread, cut into 1" cubes (about 8 slices, or 3½ cups)
Vegetable oil cooking spray
2½ cups low-fat milk
⅓ cup maple syrup (use the real stuff)
2 tablespoons granulated sugar
1 teaspoon vanilla extract
½ teaspoon or more cinnamon, to your taste
⅛ teaspoon salt
⅛ teaspoon ground nutmeg
2 egg whites
1 egg
⅓ cup brown raisins

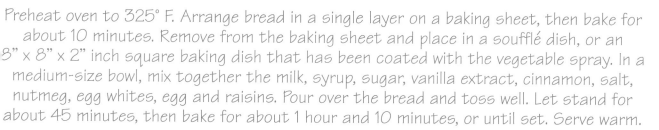

Preheat oven to 325° F. Arrange bread in a single layer on a baking sheet, then bake for about 10 minutes. Remove from the baking sheet and place in a soufflé dish, or an 8" x 8" x 2" inch square baking dish that has been coated with the vegetable spray. In a medium-size bowl, mix together the milk, syrup, sugar, vanilla extract, cinnamon, salt, nutmeg, egg whites, egg and raisins. Pour over the bread and toss well. Let stand for about 45 minutes, then bake for about 1 hour and 10 minutes, or until set. Serve warm.

Serves: 6 – 8

DESSERTS, COOKIES & SWEETS

MINIATURE PECAN TARTS

*You won't be able to eat just one of these little tarts. The cream cheese dough is rich
and flaky. The filling is nutty and sweet rolled into one. Beautiful on a tea table.
These are wonderful and freeze well.*

For the crust:
3 ounces regular or low-fat cream cheese, softened
$\frac{1}{4}$ cup butter
1 cup all-purpose flour

For the filling:
$\frac{3}{4}$ cup brown sugar, packed
1 egg, beaten
$\frac{1}{2}$ cup chopped pecans
$1\frac{1}{2}$ tablespoon melted butter
$\frac{1}{2}$ cup confectioners' sugar

Blend the crust ingredients with a pastry blender, mixing well. Chill several hours or
overnight, then press mixture into miniature muffin tins. Combine sugar, egg, pecans and
butter. Spoon into muffin tins. Bake in a preheated 350° F. oven for 20 – 25 minutes.
Cool several minutes, then dust with the confectioners' sugar.

Makes: 1 $\frac{1}{2}$ dozen

CHANGE OF PACE LEMON BARS

Lemon Bar Cookies are a change of pace and hold up well. Ah, the fresh, fragrant taste of real lemon! Although sweet, the tanginess of the lemon provides a unique ending to a meal.

$1^{1}/_{2}$ cup plus 3 tablespoons unsifted all-purpose flour
$^{1}/_{2}$ cup confectioners sugar
$^{3}/_{4}$ cup cold butter
4 eggs, slightly beaten
$1^{1}/_{2}$ cup sugar
1 teaspoon baking powder
$^{1}/_{2}$ cup lemon juice
Additional confectioners' sugar, for dusting

Preheat the oven to 350° F. In a medium-size bowl, combine 1 $^{1}/_{2}$ cups of the flour and $^{1}/_{2}$ cup confectioners sugar; cut in the butter until mixture is crumbly. Press this mixture into the bottom of a lightly greased 1 3" x 9-inch baking pan; bake 10-15 minutes until light brown. Meanwhile, in a large bowl, combine the eggs, granulated sugar, baking powder, lemon juice and the remaining 3 tablespoons flour; mix well. Pour over the baked crust; bake 20-25 minutes, or until lightly browned. Cool completely. Cut into bars and sprinkle with additional confectioners' sugar. These freeze, but don't use confectioners' sugar on the top until you completely defrost them.

Makes: About 24 bars

DESSERTS, COOKIES & SWEETS

EASY BOURBON-PECAN ICE CREAM

Here's a variation on a recipe I learned while watching one of Jacques Pepin's cooking shows. You need not tell your guests how to prepare this scrumptious dessert. Just let them go home believing you've made this fantastic ice cream all by yourself. Use low-fat ice cream, if you prefer.

1 pint (2 cups) vanilla ice cream
2 tablespoons bourbon
2 tablespoons chopped, toasted pecans

Soften the vanilla ice cream until it has a medium consistency that can be stirred. Add the bourbon and pecans. Mix well. Scoop, or pour back into the original container, or another, then refreeze. For a variations, add one or all of the following: cinnamon, 2 tablespoons of Kahlua® liqueur, and or chocolate chunks, or chips.

Serves: 4 – 6

MINIATURE FRUITY CHEESECAKES

This fruity recipe makes about three dozen miniature cheesecakes. Surprisingly, they freeze well for a month, or more. Here's another tip: when you're defrosting any of the baked goods, leave them in their container and keep covered. That way the condensation forms on the outside and the baked goods don't get gooey. Use reduced-fat cream cheese to cut down on calories.

1¹/₂ packages 8-ounce reduced-fat cream cheese
¹/₂ cup granulated sugar
2 eggs
³/₄ teaspoon vanilla extract
1 cup sour cream
¹/₄ cup granulated sugar
¹/₂ teaspoon vanilla extract
1 cup strawberry preserves

Preheat oven to 300° F. Soften the cream cheese in a medium-size bowl. Using an electric mixer, combine sugar and cream cheese thoroughly. Add the eggs one at a time, beating well. Add vanilla extract: beat until smooth and creamy. Place miniature muffin papers in muffin tins (you can also use regular muffin size) and fill two-thirds full.

Bake for 20-25 minutes, or until set. Cool for 5 minutes. Prepare the topping in another medium-size bowl by thoroughly mixing sour cream, granulated sugar, and the vanilla extract. Spoon about ¹/₂ teaspoon of this mixture on top of each miniature muffin, then top with a dab of strawberry preserves or another fruit preserve that you may prefer. Return tins to the oven and bake for another 10 minutes.

Makes: 24 - 36 dozen miniature cheesecakes

MANGO SORBET

You will impress your family with this easy, yet unique, dessert. If you haven't tried mango, make sure you do. Because it is sweet in a different sort of way, mango is difficult to define; it's like an upgraded peach. Try serving the sorbet in scooped-out orange or lemon halves, with a sprig of mint on top. You'll think you are on some far away island! And, of course, make sure you use ripe mangoes.

2 cups mango puree
1 cup water
³/₄ cups granulated sugar
1 tablespoon fresh lemon juice

Pour the water and sugar into a small saucepan, mix well and bring to a boil over medium heat. Boil 1 minute, or until sugar is dissolved. Cool well. Then add mango puree and lemon juice. Mix well and pour into an ice cream machine. Follow the directions for your ice cream machine, or freeze in ice tray in the coldest part of your freezer. If you freeze in an ice cube tray, or other dish, remove from freezer when just set and stir well with a fork. Return to freezer until ready to use.

Makes: 4 servings

NOTES

INDEX

INDEX

What the Critics Say...

"Sandy Freedman, who for years presided as Mayor over Tampa,
is now chief executive of her kitchen."
— Mary Scourtes, **The Tampa Tribune**

"The recipes are <u>great</u> for working moms!"
— Kelly Ring, **News Anchor, FOX13 News**, Tampa

"Mayor Sandy could take the political heat, as well as the kitchen heat,
and her mayoral record and cookbook prove it.
The book is a bodacious, gastronomical humdinger!"
— Jack Harris, **WFLA Newsradio 970 AM**, Tampa